HENRY ADAMS

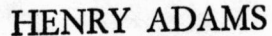

HENRY ADAMS

Drawing from life by John Briggs Potter

HENRY ADAMS

James Truslow Adams

GREENWOOD PRESS, PUBLISHERS
WESTPORT, CONNECTICUT

Originally published in 1933
by Albert & Charles Boni, Inc., New York

Reprinted from an original copy in the collections
of the Brooklyn Public Library

First Greenwood Reprinting 1970

Library of Congress Catalogue Card Number 70-109703

SBN 8371-4194-X

Printed in the United States of America

This volume is

dedicated

with respect, gratitude and affection

to

WORTHINGTON CHAUNCEY FORD

CONTENTS

LIST OF ILLUSTRATIONS

PREFACE

THIS life of Henry Adams was originally written for a
collected edition of his *Works* in many volumes. Adams
himself would have enjoyed the irony of the fact that the
very break-down of our economic system—whether temporary or not—which he predicted a generation before
it occurred has precluded the possibility of publishing
his own *Works* for the time being on the scale contem-
plated. There is no reason, however, for withholding
longer from publication the only biography of him which
has yet been written.

The author wishes to extend cordial thanks for help
received to Mr. Worthington C. Ford, Mr. William
Adams Slade, Mr. Leonard L. Mackall, Mr. William A.
Jackson, Mr. Henry Osborn Taylor, Mrs. L. H. Thoron,
the Massachusetts Historical Society and, as always, to
the staff of the Library of Congress. He also wishes to
thank Messrs. Houghton Mifflin Company for permission
to quote from *The Education of Henry Adams*.

—J. T. A.

THE HERITAGE

THE HERITAGE

1.

THE HERITAGE

"UNDER the shadow of Boston State House, turning its back on the house of John Hancock, the little passage called Hancock Avenue runs, or ran, from Beacon Street, skirting the State House grounds, to Mount Vernon Street, on the summit of Beacon Hill; and there, in the third house below Mount Vernon Place, February 16, 1838, a child was born, and christened later by his uncle, the minister of the First Church after the tenets of Boston Unitarianism, as Henry Brooks Adams. Had he been born in Jerusalem under the shadow of the Temple and circumcised in the Synagogue by his uncle the high priest, under the name of Israel Cohen, he would scarcely have been more distinctly branded, and not much more heavily handicapped in the races of the coming century, in running for such stakes as the century was to offer." [1]

Thus, characteristically, did Adams at the beginning of *The Education* narrate the facts, heavy with implications, of his own birth. He was, indeed, heavily ticketed, as he says, with safeguards, safeguards such as, he believed, would have ensured any young man's success a century earlier. That the safeguards had a profound influence upon his outward career and inner life is obvious. Whether they were helps or hindrances to success would depend largely upon what that success should be considered to consist of. In spite of the long sustained irony of *The Education,* it is certain that he never would willingly have dispensed with them. "Probably no child, born in the year, held better cards than he," was his own comment when more than three score years of his life had been lived out.

[1] All quotations, when not otherwise specified, are from *The Education of Henry Adams.* The author thanks Messrs. Houghton Mifflin Company for permission to make the extracts.

Disregarding for the present his statement that he never got to the point of playing the game, let us look at the cards which composed what he admitted to be one of the most excellent hands a player could hold. There was scarcely a card below a ten spot, and almost all the picture cards were ancestral portraits.

There were back of Adams seven generations of ancestors but only three of portraits. What suddenly transformed a succession of deuces of spades into an equally continuous succession of kings of diamonds is an unsolvable riddle. Perhaps it was Susanna Boylston. At any rate, about 1609 a certain Henry Adams of yeoman stock and a copyholder of the manor of Barton Saint David, Somersetshire, England, married a certain Edith Squire of Charlton Mackrell in the same county, and, about seventeen years later, the couple, with their son Joseph and eight other children, emigrated to Massachusetts and settled at Braintree, then known as Mount Wollaston. If this first Henry left property of but small value,—it totalled about £75 including the house, land, and barn, the cow and the pigs,—nevertheless at his death he had firmly planted his family in the stubborn soil of Massachusetts Bay and left them two items of note,—a few books and a silver spoon. The son, Joseph (1626-1694), was a maltster and selectman, and left two sons, Joseph the elder and John. John claims a moment's attention as the grandfather of Samuel of Revolutionary fame but our concern is with Joseph (1654-1737). He married Hannah Bass, was a selectman, and father of Deacon John (1691-1764), who was a farmer and shoemaker, and married Susanna Boylston. It would seem to have been a rather brilliant match for the farmer-shoemaker. Susanna came of a family prominent in the medical history of the colony and apparently was endowed with a better quality of mind than had hitherto been noticeable in the Adams strain. With their eldest son, John (1735-1826), the portraits and the remarkable mental qualities of the family make their appearance. The family also begins, as it will thenceforth continue to be, international in relations, intermittent residence, preoccupation, and influence.

John would loom portentously large in any family line. Possibly the most important member of the Continental Congress; a commissioner to negotiate peace with England; the first minister of the newly independent United States to that country; Vice-President of the United States twice and President once; he lifted the family from provincial obscurity to an international rank and an international outlook. His greatest services and successes all stemmed from his activities as an opponent of British policy. A self-made man, although of consummate ability, he had some of the characteristics of that type in high degree, including jealousy, self-confidence, extreme egotism and vanity. Ambitious, he loved power and was at his best in action, although an omnivorous student and with a mind heavily stored. A statesman always, he never succeeded as a politician, his virtues as well as defects precluding success in that trade. He was fascinated by constitutional problems; possessed a strong historical imagination; and was a voluminous author.

A famous father, if a "safeguard" for some careers is not seldom "an old man of the sea" for others, particularly that in which the father has shone. In this case, however, the son, John Quincy (1767-1848), ran an even better race than his father along curiously similar lines. The oldest son of John and his extraordinarily able wife, the celebrated letter-writer, Abigail Smith, granddaughter of the Rev. John Norton, the boy began his international experiences at the age of ten by accompanying his father when the latter went on the French mission in 1778. He studied at Paris, Leyden and The Hague; was secretary to the United States Minister to Russia, and to his own father during the peace negotiations with England, before he returned to America to graduate at Harvard and study law like his father before him. Soon appointed Minister to the Netherlands by Washington, he negotiated a treaty at Berlin, and

JOHN QUINCY ADAMS
Portrait by Gilbert Stuart, 1818

married in London Louisa Johnson of both English and Maryland blood. Among other offices held by him were those of United States Senator, Minister to Russia, a member of the Commission to negotiate peace with England in 1813; first United States Minister to England after the war; Secretary of State; President of the United States; and member of Congress for seventeen years, winning there perhaps his most enduring fame in his long struggle for the right of petition. He was as omnivorous a student and an even more voluminous writer than his father. Deeply conscientious, both religiously and intellectually, it has been said that he would leave "no argument without exhausting its possibility." A greater statesman than his father, he was, like him, a failure as a politician. Like him also he was pugnacious, often bitterly vindictive in expression, and yet had a strong strain of tenderness. Unlike his father, however, whose interests, wide as they were, centered mainly in history, jurisprudence, statesmanship and philosophy, John Quincy developed an intense interest and considerable ability in science, made notable among other ways in his *Report on Weights and Measures* and his constant efforts to assist American astronomy. Here again, as an ancestor, was a "safeguard" or an old man of the sea as case and career might prove.

Charles Francis (1807-1886), the son of John Quincy and father of Henry, began his international and diplomatic experience even younger than his father, who took the boy with him to St. Petersburg at the age of two. At eight, after thoroughly mastering French, he was taken by his mother by carriage across Europe in the winter of 1815 in time to be in Paris for the "Hundred Days" on his way to England, which was the then diplomatic post of John Quincy. Schooling in England and Boston, graduation from Harvard, and some study in the law office of Daniel Webster followed, as did also his marriage to Abigail Brown, daughter of Peter Chardon Brooks, an extremely wealthy Boston merchant of that day. Hitherto the Adamses, who had never bothered to make money, had had but little of it. They had not in truth needed it, for their tastes were even more simple than the times and they had had most of what the world can give, without it. Without a larger share of it than the earlier generations had enjoyed, however, the career of Henry would have been different. Indeed, the glorious late career of John Quincy was only made possible by the care which his son gave to the little property the old man had. Charles ran for Vice-President in 1848 but was defeated, and the weight of accumulated ancestry began to tell in his devoting his next eight years to editing the *Works* of his grandfather and writing his *Life*. He was to prove, however, the greatest diplomatist in the family, and, after serving in Congress, he sailed in 1861 to take up his post as United States Minister in England, where, with Henry as private secretary, he remained until 1868. Three years later he was United States Arbitrator at Geneva in the Alabama Claims case.

Here, then, were some of the cards that the "ten pounds of unconscious babyhood," as Adams calls himself on that sixteenth of February, 1838, held in its tiny fingers in the house on Hancock Avenue,—two Presidents; three Ministers to England; two Commissioners to negotiate peace with England; any number of Congressional and Senatorial terms; various foreign missions; three reputations in letters and scholarship; any amount of foreign residence and education; no haunting financial worry; assured social reputation on two continents; three wars made or largely controlled by his family; a national history inextricably intertwined with his own; inherited traits, good and bad, of a most pronounced sort. The cradle must fairly have groaned, if the infant did not, under the accumulated weight.

I shall not here attempt any biological inferences as to Adams's inheritance nor Freudian guesses as to his childhood. We know too little as yet of all that. Adams's brother Brooks, in his long essay on *The Heritage of Henry Adams,* claims that Henry, intellectually, stemmed directly from his grandfather, old John Quincy, finding precisely

the same "caste of intelligence,"—the scientific
mixed with the political,—in each. Henry, in turn,
accounts in part for himself as a survival of his
grandmother, John Quincy's wife, the somewhat
delicate exotic whom her stronger mother-in-law,
Abigail, had feared would never adjust herself to
the rigors of the New England physical and mental
climates. "She was Louis Seize, like the furniture,"
wrote Adams of his youthful recollections. "The
boy knew nothing of her interior life, which had
been, as the venerable Abigail, long since at peace,
foresaw, one of severe stress and little pure satisfaction. He never dreamed that from her might come
some of those doubts and self-questionings, those
hesitations, those rebellions against law and discipline, which marked more than one of her
descendants; but he might even then have felt
some vague instinctive suspicion that he was to in-
herit from her the seeds of the primal sin, the fall
from grace, the curse of Abel, that he was not of
pure New England stock, but half exotic."

If, however, we trouble neither the reader nor

ourselves with vague gropings after Mendelian or other laws, mere human experience will tell us that such an inheritance as Adams's was not to be lightly borne. As he himself said, "one had to pay for Revolutionary patriots; grandfathers and grandmothers; Presidents; diplomats; Queen Anne mahogany and Louis Seize chairs, as well as for Stuart portraits." Quite apart from other equally obvious effects they would, in America, almost indubitably prevent the inheritor from pursuing a career and from achieving any consciousness of success in any career chosen. A scion of a family that had lived in a perpetual feud for three distinguished generations with the banking and business interests as represented in State Street, could hardly aim at commercial success without a haunting sense of betrayal of the family ideals and history. If one thought of a public career, not only were modern conditions against the emergence of a pure statesman but any political life that stopped below the presidency could not but prove a failure as compared with one's grandfather and great-grandfather. In diplo-

macy it would be the same. Any post to be
achieved could not but look small as compared
with the two peace negotiations of 1783 and 1814,
with the three ministries to England at critical moments in history. Adams's own temporary service
as secretary to his father when Minister in London
during the Civil War would have also stood in the
way. As he said later, "any one who had held,
during the four most difficult years of American
diplomacy, a position at the center of action, with
his hands actually touching the lever of power,
could not beg a post of Secretary at Vienna or
Madrid in order to bore himself doing nothing
until the next President should do him the honor
to turn him out." In any case, the family holding of the highest posts at the most critical
moments for three generations would be bound
to make the holding of any lower ones by a
descendant assume the aspect of failure or de-
generation. Moreover, there was the point that
the family, since it had been a "family," had always had its hand "on the lever of power." When

one has controlled power it is not easy to yield it. The sense of wielding it gets into one's blood. When, in a modern democracy, one's family has held it for a century, the situation becomes intolerably difficult. With such an inheritance, a certain miasmatic air of failure would be bound to hang about a law office, a doctor's receiving room or even a historian's study, unless the last were not merely the ante-room to a wider world. Thus almost any achievement below the grade of the very highest, and that in the line of power, to be won in the future by the infant we have left sleeping his first sleep in 1838 would come to seem very much like sniping at bull frogs in Walden Pond to a son, grandson and great-grandson of men who had fought lions, tigers and elephants in the jungle. It might be amusing but could hardly be regarded seriously as success.

Of his large family of brothers and sisters, he says that unconscious as their development may have been in many ways, they were all conscious of wishing to control power in some form. The obvious form for them was politics or literature. The ancestors had always exerted it in a combination of both. Apparently it never occurred to Adams that literature divorced from activity in other lines is extremely apt to bring about a feeling of frustration. In his own case, with background and inheritance of a public wielding of power through the State, almost any competent adviser, even quite devoid of modern psychology, could have warned him that it would almost inevitably do so for him.

Adams made much of the fact that in spiritual and mental outlook he was "an eighteenth century child." Apart from any obscure biological principles at work, we may note that with a family so heavily weighted with that century on his back, Adams would, in America, have found it difficult to be anything else. Given the inheritance, it was in a way a misfortune that it was American, though no American family would have more quickly resented the suggestion. Had, however, Adams's ancestors held correspondingly important positions in England, say the most important of missions and diplomatic posts for three generations and prime minister for two, the family influence, power and prestige would have steadily grown, and had the young Henry displayed ability and inclination for public life, opportunity for such a career would have come to him abundantly. What would have been inestimable advantages in the England of Victoria were crushing weights in the United States of Ulysses S. Grant. In addition, we may note that even a peerage, which would probably have been bestowed upon the family in England, would merely have placed them among their "peers." To have established, on the other hand, a sort of hereditary aristocracy of three generations, albeit of intellect and temporary public office, in one family in a democracy otherwise notable for rather chaotic individualism, was to court the danger of exaggerated self-consciousness. Even a duke finds other dukes to temper the exaltation of his social station. But a family which maintains power and prestige generation after generation in the shifting sands of democratic life, where otherwise power and prestige inhere only in individuals, may reach the wasteful and distressing situation in which the democracy does not know what to do with the family and the family does not know what to do with itself. The rather pretty problem involves evils the exact reverse of those that may crop up in a government by hereditary aristocrats.

BOYHOOD

2.

BOYHOOD

OF Adams's boyhood we need not recall much.
He gives an incomparable picture of it in his
Education, to which the reader may turn. We need
here note only one or two points. For one, at three
years of age he had an extremely severe case of
scarlet fever which may well have exerted a continued influence throughout life. The entire Adams
tribe were and always had been short in height, but
Adams says that his illness resulted in stunting his
growth so that he was two or three inches below
his brothers. Mere physical size seems frequently
to have psychological results or concomitants,
though we should not lay too much stress upon
what is so obscure. Adams, however, was always

nervous and high-strung, shy and sensitive to a high degree. The severe illness, which nearly ended fatally, superimposed upon his inheritance, may have helped shape his make-up and outlook.

His childhood held many contrasts which he has himself elaborated. The New England seasons,—the effort to live in winter and the tropical license of summer,—were hardly more opposed than the splendor of his grandfather Brooks's house in town and the eighteenth century simplicity of the old Adams house at Quincy, where, still a living figure for the boy, dwelt the venerable President grandfather, John Quincy. There was the usual schooling, but overheard conversation must have had far more influence upon him than schoolrooms. For most men to say, in looking back at the boy they had been, that by ten "his face was already fixed, and his heart was stone, against State Street; his education was warped beyond recovery in the direction of Puritan politics," would be considered an amiable exaggeration. We must recall, however, not only that the young Adams was living in

HENRY BROOKS ADAMS, AS AN UNDERGRADUATE

the Boston of Emerson, Garrison, Webster, Phillips,
Channing, Prescott, Lowell, Holmes, Longfellow,
and the rest of the varied galaxy of the 1840's, many
of whom were acquaintances, though only a few
close friends, of his father, but that among the
friends, most intimate at the house, were Palfrey,
Dana and Charles Sumner, the last being the
boy's idol. Living among such surroundings in
the winter, in the house at 57 Mount Vernon
Street into which his father had moved in 1842,
and with old John Quincy at Quincy in the
summers, the boy's mind may easily have taken
on a firm complexion by ten, an age when
most American boys of the day would have
heard little or nothing worth listening to in
their homes. In 1848, the boy's father ran for
Vice-President on the ticket of the Free Soil party,
and the boy was initiated into politics in a way to
come home to him very directly. He had a writing table in his father's library and there, while
doing his Latin grammar, he listened to discussions
on the questions of the day between his father, Pal-

frey, Dana and Sumner. Probably no other American boy has had such a running accompaniment to *hic, hæc, hoc*.

The Free Soil party having been defeated, the father betook himself to the editing of the *Works* of his grandfather, the President John Adams, and the boy read the proof. In addition, he became an insatiable reader of anything he chose among his father's books, mostly eighteenth century history, and of the "new" authors, such as Dickens and Thackeray then coming out, Dickens remaining a favorite with him throughout life. He also, he says, read shelves full of eighteenth century poetry, though his late strong taste for Wordsworth did not develop until he was thirty. Scott was swallowed whole, and the father read aloud Tennyson and much else to the children in the evenings. They also joined in the lively discussions at the dinner table and "were accustomed to hear," as Adams tells us, "almost every day, table-talk as good as they were ever likely to hear again," an encomium that can be appreciated only when we realize that in later life Henry was to sit at many of the best tables on both sides of the Atlantic. Because of the extreme rarification of the religious atmosphere in the Unitarian Boston, and household, of 1850, Adams considers that "so one-sided an education could have been possible in no other country or time," but whether his emotional life would have been enriched in that quarter by having been, say, an acolyte in the cathedral of Chartres, we cannot determine. Whatever æsthetic or religious emotions Adams was to feel later, he was essentially an intellectual, and his education in this respect, while it may have influenced, probably did not seriously warp, his real nature.

When twelve years old a more important educational episode occurred in the form of a visit to Washington, in May, 1850. After his grandfather's sudden death in Congress in 1848 his wife, "the Madam" as she was called, remained in her Washington home, and it was she with whom the boy stayed. The youngster was taken to the Senate and introduced to many of the Senators, as well as to the White House, where all his family had lived at one time or another, and where he met President Taylor, an intimate family friend. He took instinctively to the shambling, rambling town that Washington then was, on the banks of the Potomac, but the immediate contact with slavery on the one hand, and, on the other, a visit to Mount Vernon, the home of the greatest of Americans and a slaveholder, started questionings. Life began to appear more complex, though a boy's mind easily holds contradictions. Slavery, however, threw him back on Puritanism and assumed the sixteenth century rôles of Stuart kings and Roman pontiffs. His "first vague sense of feeling an unknown living obstacle in the dark came in 1851," he tells us, in trying to reconcile sixteenth century principles, the eighteenth century statesmanship of his family, and nineteenth century party organization and methods in politics.

For his formal education, Adams always expressed contempt, and Harvard fared little better in this respect than the bitterly resented school of

Mr. Bixwell in Bedford Street. He entered Harvard in 1854 and for the first two years lived outside the college buildings in a room which he shared with his elder brother, Charles Francis, Junior, during the latter's Junior and Senior years. The brother says that when he graduated he persuaded Henry to live in one of the college dormitories and to take a chum of his own class, identifying himself with the college life and the associations of Holworthy; and that the advice saved the course for Henry. Henry, however, never shared the belief that he had been saved. In fact, he later debated with himself the problem whether Harvard had not ruined him. "It taught little," he wrote, "and that little ill," and the whole four years' work could easily have been put into four months of any later period of life. From his college mates, he claims to have got little or nothing, though they included such young men as Phillips Brooks, Alexander Agassiz, H. H. Richardson, and Oliver Wendell Holmes, the younger. The small Southern group, including a son of Robert E.

Lee, appears to have interested him more, because of the greater difference in type from that to which he was used. If he got slight advantage from his fellows he considers that he got no more from his teachers. In a word, it was his opinion that the four years were wasted. Inheritance could not help but play its part in the failure. Unlike so many, he was in no need of the social air of the college. It was no better, if as good, as that he had always breathed outside it; and a young man who since childhood had listened to the familiar talk of men like his father and grandfather, Palfrey, Sumner and the rest, could not but find rather futile the classroom lectures by less eminent men, intended for immature minds that had not been in intimate touch with those of presidents, statesmen, philosophers and historians. From James Russell Lowell, fresh from the German universities, he did indeed get something, and that something led him to his first step onward into the international world. He determined himself to try Germany. When he graduated in 1858 he had got all an American university of that day could give him. He had made his first start in literature by articles in the *Harvard Magazine*. He had been Class Orator and by means of various activities, including acting in the comedies of the Hasty Pudding Club, had acquired ease in public speaking. He was ready, as he notes, to stand up before any audience in America with his nerves rather the steadier for the excitement.

As one thinks of him at this point in his career, however, one realizes an inherent weakness in his position. He might speak before any audience in America but he did not know or understand that audience. He had lived too exclusively with minds of the highest order to have any sympathetic understanding of minds of an inferior order, and it was those minds that were to control the dispensing of positions of power. An eighteenth century statesman was hopelessly lost in the rough hurly-burly of nineteenth century politics. Every increase in the electorate had entailed a corresponding increase in coarseness of fiber for those who would ascend to power by means of popular election. If Adams were ever to hold power, the education, given his nature and inheritance, that he needed was an education in coarsening. So far, every step in that education, formal or informal, had been a step in the direction of greater refinement, emotional and intellectual. There might, indeed, have yet been time. A few years earlier another young Bostonian, similarly handicapped by his inheritance, though to a far lesser extent, Richard Henry Dana, had tempered that inheritance to the uses of a public career by two years before the mast. To his knowledge of Harrison Gray Otis's drawing room Dana added that of the fo'castle. If he moved easily among the Ticknors, Eliots, Guilds, Nortons, Longfellows, Howes, Lymans, Appletons, Prescotts and Wards, to list those at one afternoon gathering, he moved no less so among the riff-raff of common sailors with very different surnames or none. Instead, however, of sailing for California as a deckhand, young Adams embarked, in November, 1858, for a German university in the largest, newest and most luxurious steamship then afloat, as a first-class passenger.

YOUTH AND EUROPE

3.

YOUTH AND EUROPE

ONE does not have to be the captious critic Adams suggests to assert that the Adams family owed all they were to Europe. Through three generations, what they were always pleased to consider the stupidities of Europe had given them the opportunity of shining themselves. Of his immediate ancestors, the first had gone to Europe at forty-three, the second at eight and the third at two years of age. According to the mathematical laws of which Henry was so fond, he should himself have thus gone at six months. He might have calculated that his delaying until he was twenty marked a certain degradation in the family energy or decreased adaptation to environment. In any

[53]

case, considering his inheritance from the past on the one hand and the jungle of nineteenth century politics on the other, in view of that desire to control power in some form which could be the only touchstone of success for an Adams, we cannot but feel as we watch him ascend the gang-plank of the *Persia* that November day, headed for Berlin instead of San Francisco, that the game is up. The past has been too much for him. He is walking backward toward it, a solitary figure, while the motley horde of the dispensers of power in the future are pressing forward in a disorderly rush toward the Golden Gate. Inheritance and education have made him impotent to join. Two years of Europe will make him less so. Seven years more will end all possibility. One of my own great-uncles spent seventeen years in Paris studying how to be useful to his native land in South America only to be exiled by a half-breed revolution when he got there. Henry's position was not dissimilar. He was to achieve a success and a distinction that would have been ample for anyone without his inheritance but which with that inheritance could not but spell failure for him. He was never to have his hand on the lever of power. His dream, however, was to persist for another dozen years until he felt it shattered by the coarse hand of Grant. Looking back now from the assured vantage ground of seventy years later, with Henry's inheritance, temperament, and the course of our national history open to us, we can see, as he did not, that, for him, the dead hand of the past had emptied the dream of all reality long before he saw that of Grant outstretched.

He was, indeed, to receive a marvellous training, but it was not one leading to late nineteenth century power. He quickly discovered on the steamer the truth that "a great many impressions were needed to make a very little education." The collecting of impressions and the handing of them on to others, impressions of history, of science, of art, of society, of the past, of the future, were to constitute Henry's distinct work. It was to lead to one of the greatest contributions any one man of letters has made to American intellectual life. But it was not to lead to power.

His voyage apparently lasted about a month and provided for his education seasickness, a first-class November gale, and G. P. R. James. Adams landed at Liverpool, visited Eaton Hall, and found that both aristocracy and the England of Dickens were real. On the way to London, the train passed through the Black District but although this might also have provided education, "the boy," he tells us, "ran away from it, as he ran away from everything he disliked." From London and the eighteenth century, he passed to Antwerp and the sixteenth, an Antwerp still medieval, without tourists and without sanitation. Even Rubens and the Descent from the Cross seemed modern to the young man who there tasted "one of the fullest and strongest flavors" that had yet touched his palate.

In the spring when he had delivered his Oration at Harvard one of his eminent uncles had remarked that for a young man it was singularly wanting in enthusiasm. In an unsympathetic essay upon him

JOHN ADAMS, IN OLD AGE

Portrait by Gilbert Stuart, 1823

after his death, Gamaliel Bradford questioned how deeply he might ever really have felt either religion, nature or art. Adams himself says that at Antwerp he "got drunk on his emotions, and had then to get sober as best he could." The significance of the remark depends, of course, on how strong a head for emotion he had. It is somewhat illuminated by an experience at Berlin, where he soon arrived. He had, as he says, never so much as listened to music in his life, and that daily provided for him in the beer-gardens did not awaken any sense until one day he suddenly discovered, inattentively, that he was following a symphony of Beethoven. At that moment, he tells us, "a new sense burst out like a flower in his life, so superior to the old senses, so bewildering, so astonished at its own existence, that he could not credit it, and," as he significantly adds, he "watched it as something apart, accidental, and not to be trusted." Wagner, the early Wagner, also came to be somewhat "intelligible" to him, although he was sixty before he appreciated the Götterdämmerung. We have al-

ready noted that he was thirty before he felt Wordsworth. To the end of his life, he tells in another
place, he never "felt a sense of majesty in French
verse." Yet again, he says that as he approached
sixty, the artist began to die and only an intense
cerebral restlessness survived,—"one was driven
from beauty to beauty as though art was a trotting
match." Always a great reader and a frequent
quoter of poetry, one cannot escape the conclusion
after one has lived with his writing for a long time,
that it was thought, rather than emotion, which
ever made the stronger appeal to him, and that he
treated the latter, as he did his sudden pleasure in
Beethoven, as "something apart, accidental, and not
to be trusted." Three generations of European
contacts at high points had not undone the bleak
work of Massachusetts Bay, and to understand
Henry sitting in the Berlin beer-garden, distrustful
of the unexpected, and one almost feels, unwelcome
thrills sent along his spine by Beethoven, one has
to hark back to the first Henry in his four room
house on the barren soil of Puritan Mount Wollas-

ton. Whatever Adams's trip to Europe was to be, it was evidently not to be an adventure among masterpieces, in spite, in years to come, of Chartres and Mont-Saint-Michel.

The ostensible object of it had been the study of the Civil Law. That his mind should have turned to the law was almost inevitable. The feud with State Street, and other reasons, pointed to a profession being essential where business was out of the question. An Adams as either clergyman or doctor was unthinkable, and each of his three immediate ancestors had been members of the bar. It was the fittest glove for one's hand when gripping the lever of power. Why, however, he should have pursued the Civil Law as far as Berlin is somewhat obscure. At any rate, he did not find it there, though he did run across Charles Sumner. His first lecture was his last. He discovered that he would have to learn the language first and that the despised Harvard "was instinct with life as compared with all that he could see of the University of Berlin," the mental attitude of which, he not un-

naturally found, "was not of an American world."
With all sympathy for the bewildered young man,
one cannot suppress wondering why, if he was in
search of an American world, he did not look for
it under his nose in State Street instead of in
Unter den Linden. The Prussian government, he
found, did not, under Bismarck and the Regent,
encourage reasoning.

Berlin became a nightmare to him, and when
some friend suggested a tramp in Thuringia in
April, his "heart sang like a bird." The four
tramps, however—the other three, Boston and
Harvard like himself,—had had enough of the
open road in twenty-four hours, and moved into
comfortable quarters severally at Dresden. As
throwing light on the value he set on æsthetic emotion, his comment on the new venture is illuminating enough, even allowing for irony. "There was
nothing to study" there, he notes, "and no education to be gained, but the Sistine Madonna and the
Correggios were famous; the theater and opera were
sometimes excellent, and the Elbe was prettier

than the Spree." *C'est tout.* It is true that this was written in old age when irony had become a pose, and that he spoke in a letter to his brother from Dresden of "the Madonna, the most exquisite of all exquisiteness."[1] Dresden lasted for a few months, until, in July, 1859, Adams went to join his sister, Mrs. Charles Kuhn, at Thun in Switzerland. The scenery, although as "famous" in its way as the Sistine Madonna and the Correggios, seems to have meant little to him. He suggests that there may have been a first impression but comments, again illuminatingly, that he "never afterwards cared much for landscape education, except perhaps in the tropics for the sake of the contrast. As education, that chapter, too, was read, and set aside." A person who finds genuine sources of emotional satisfaction does not so cavalierly set them aside.

War, of course, was on in '59 and the party crossed the frontier between the opposing lines,

[1] *Letters of Henry Adams, 1858-1891*, edited by Worthington Chauncey Ford, Boston, 1930, p. 44.

making its way northward again into Germany where Adams says he "conscientiously did his cathedrals, his Rhine, and whatever his companions suggested." The Rhine is rather a disappointing stream but it must be confessed that we find this boy of twenty-one in Europe, as did his uncle at Harvard, "singularly wanting in enthusiasm." Determined, however, to carry out his plan of pursuing the Civil Law in Germany, he passed the next winter in Dresden, apparently without much of either satisfaction or profit, and then, turning frankly tourist, went to Italy, joining his sister once more, at Florence in April, 1860. Of the ten pages which he devotes in the *Education* to the Italian episode, there is not a word of art or nature, which at that period we may conclude he considered, or pretended to consider, negligible for the purposes of his spirit.

The record of the boy's mind in *The Education* is set down by a man of nearly three score and ten. Much, of course, must be allowed for that and for the disdains and disgusts developed in the course of a long and fastidious life-time. But to a great extent the letters written to his family and most intimate friends in these early European years merely confirm the impression received from the later retrospect. Writing to his brother, Charles Francis, when thirty-one, he noted that his brother liked "roughness and strength" whereas "I like taste and dexterity."[1] A love of "taste and dexterity" is scarcely the spiritual equipment for the development of a genuinely deep and moving appreciation of either great scenery or great art, though it is entirely compatible with a high degree of æsthetic interest of a sort. Adams's taste and tastes developed, as do those of any essentially civilized man, throughout his life, but we find him continually subordinating art and æsthetic emotion to reason in an untiring quest for intellectual knowledge. He admits the power exerted by Venus and the Virgin but his own particular problem is how to correlate those powers with that of the dynamo. Among those who knew him well, I find a difference of

[1] *Letters,* cit supra, p. 160.

opinion, the women stressing his love of art and beauty whereas the men insist that he was essentially the intellectual. It may be said only, by one who never met him, that the opinion of the latter is the one borne out by the great mass of writings which he left, ranging from those intended for the public to those meant only for the eyes of most intimate friends.

Just what the boy may have been groping for in Europe, it is impossible to say. Probably, hampered by inheritance and Boston, he was trying to have a good time and also to prepare himself seriously in some way for his future. It has been said that Adams wrote five hundred pages called *Education* and never defined the word. Such a statement as this can be due only to careless reading, for to a diligent reader his idea comes out clearly enough. If he never found a satisfactory method of education he has succinctly expressed his own idea of its aim and of the test of its success. Its eternal task, he says, is to solve the problem "of running order through chaos, direction through space, discipline through freedom, unity through multiplicity." Again, he says, that it is the process that enables a man to take the stamp of his time. The fitness of the method employed "can be known only from its success." He has left us, as it happens, in no doubt as to what he considered success or at least what he was willing to record himself for all time as so considering. Looking at all the educated men he knew, he picked William C. Whitney as the one who had achieved the greatest measure of that success which should be at once the aim and the standard of education. "Already in 1893," he wrote, Whitney, who had owed his free hand to a wealthy marriage, "had finished with politics after having gratified every ambition, and swung the country almost at his will; he had thrown away the usual objects of political ambition like the ashes of smoked cigarettes; had turned to other amusements, satisfied every taste, gorged every appetite, won every object that New York afforded, and, not yet satisfied, had carried his field of activity abroad, until New York no longer knew what most to envy, his horses or his houses. He had succeeded precisely where Clarence King had failed." This vision of success and the aim of education, which comes so strangely in his old age from the descendant of the Adamses, may have been but vaguely present to the boy in Italy in 1859. That it should have been the belief of the man of sixty-odd probably means, however, that the germs at least were present in the youth, and throughout his early manhood one need neither endeavor to interpret dreams nor to poke surreptitiously in the subconscious to find that his aim was power, power of some sort over the age in which he lived, power to mold and win.

In any case, he enjoyed himself immensely in his first Italian spring. "The happiest month of May that life had yet offered." "Italy was mostly an emotion," he wrote later, "and the emotion naturally centered in Rome," even though, as he says elsewhere, "it was the worst spot in the world to teach nineteenth-century youth what to do with a twentieth-century world." The problems of time-sequence, continuity and the other unsolvable riddles of history were quite naturally roused and left unanswered. He wrote long letters to his brother, which were duly published in the *Boston Courier,* and, passing on to Naples, he had the interesting experience of being sent by the American Minister to carry dispatches to an American war-ship at Palermo, involving an interview with Garibaldi, an account of which was likewise printed in the *Courier.* Disliking everything French, he nevertheless drifted up for three pleasant months to Paris, and then, having stayed as long as he dared, took ship for home, where, in his own phrase, he "dropped back on Quincy like a lump of lead."

THE AMATEUR DIPLOMAT

4.

THE AMATEUR DIPLOMAT

URING Adams's absence his father had been elected to Congress. The boy came home to the turmoil of confusion immediately preceding the Civil War, arriving in October, 1860. A few weeks later he left for Washington with his family, reaching that city December 1st, three days before the opening of Congress, and three weeks after the election of Lincoln. During the session he acted as private secretary to his father and at its close returned with his family to Boston to study law in the office of Horace Gray. Probably while in Washington he wrote an account of the political currents of the time which long considered lost, was published as

"The Secession Winter, 1860-1861" in the *Proceedings* of the Massachusetts Historical Society just fifty years later.

He was not to remain at his desk in Gray's office. The family left Washington on the 13th of March, 1861, and on the 18th, Lincoln appointed Charles Francis Adams Minister to England, the news reaching Boston the next day. The new Minister delayed sailing until May 1st so as to be present at the marriage of his son, John Quincy, April 29th, and when he did sail he took Henry with him as private secretary. The seven years that followed in London, Adams considered either as the most interesting in retrospect of his life or the most important for his *Education,* for to them he devotes more than a third of that volume covering his whole three score and ten. Told there with such detail and in inimitable style, there is no need to repeat the story here, and we will confine ourselves to noting a few facts and making a few comments.

The attitude of England and the course of action she might take were so uncertain, the international

CHARLES FRANCIS ADAMS

situation so delicate, that for long the family of the new Minister considered that any month might be the last of their stay. After some months a lease was taken of 5 Upper Portland Place, and there, most unexpectedly to themselves, they remained until July, 1868. If the action of the British government were to remain in doubt, crisis following crisis, the feeling of most of the upper classes and many of the leading newspapers, such as the *Times,* was no matter of doubt at all. Heretofore, Henry had moved in a social atmosphere in which his claims to acceptance were so well-known as to make social life as simple a process as breathing. He had, in fact, in spite of his European experiences and his winter in Washington, hardly got beyond the purlieus of Harvard, Boston, and Quincy. Always laying much stress on social experience, it is rather noteworthy that during his first trip of two years in Europe he mentions scarcely a name as that of a person he had met except his sister, Sumner, a few Harvard classmates, and old friends. Coming from probably the most international family in America he had apparently not been furnished with a single letter of introduction of any significance, and did not meet a single well-known person, save the chance encounter with Garibaldi.

In London, as the son of the American Minister he was now to be thrown into contact with English society, such as it then was, just at a time when it was bitterly hostile on the whole to everything for which his Minister-father stood. Speaking once of the social ostracism which Sumner had encountered in Boston, Adams noted that it left him nothing to think of but himself and reacted seriously upon his character. Obviously an American Minister could not be ostracized, much less one whose father and grandfather had held similar credentials to the Court of St. James, and each of whom had been President of the United States. Nevertheless, in spite of a few powerful friends to the Minister and the Northern cause, the strong cotton and Southern sympathies of most of the upper classes during the war made the social atmosphere in spots fairly glacial in temperature, and

Henry for the first time in his life found the air in drawing rooms hostile.[1] He was of an extremely shy, sensitive, reticent and apprehensive nature, and the, so to say, spiritual ostracism that he feared rather than met in the first few years of his English experience could hardly fail to exert, as he had noted in the case of Boston and Sumner, a serious effect upon him. As a private character he might have fought or fled, but although without official position himself, he was the son of the Minister and as such had to face the drawing rooms. He says that never in his life did he labor so hard to learn a language as he then did to hold his tongue, and that the effect upon his innate reticence was permanent. The effect upon other aspects of his sensi-

[1] A son of Thomas Bayley Potter (a prominent Union sympathizer in England at that time) tells me he knew Henry well at that period, and that he much exaggerated the social isolation of the minister and the political isolation of his country. When Adams published his *Education*, Mr. Potter wrote to him stating that he felt he was doing a great deal of harm by giving such an unfair picture, and recalled to Henry a long list of men, like his father T. B. Potter, who had stood by the North at great personal sacrifice. Adams replied that he was too old to change the book and that he rather thought his own recollection correct. In any case he "couldn't bother."

tive nature, though unnoticed by him, were probably no less deep and real.

The years were passed in what was, indeed, a sensed atmosphere of hostility to his country rather than to himself. The hundred and sixteen pages devoted to the English episode betray constant irritation with his surroundings yet there are innumerable asides which indicate that the English were, on the whole, more than decent to the family of the representative of a power with which they were out of sympathy. The first twelve months were the hardest, yet Adams admits that "though at other periods of life he was sufficiently and even amply snubbed by Englishmen, he could never recall a single occasion during this trying year, when he had to complain of rudeness." Perhaps, given all the circumstances, a young man similarly placed, would have been unable to force such a confession from himself in any other country. He went "everywhere,'"—to Lord Palmerston's, Lord John Russell's, and a host of other houses, town and country,—as a matter of course. For some years, until the irregularity became too glaring, the government even did him the courtesy of allowing him to be received at Court as an attaché of the Legation, though he was in fact merely a private gentleman. His acquaintances included such men as Cobden, Bright, Monckton Milnes, Lyell, and the whole host who jostle against one another in the pages of the *Education,* "a thousand people, great and small" as he says. He even made life-long friends of an intimate sort among Milnes Gaskell and his fellow undergraduates then just starting out in life. He met many of the leading statesmen, most of the literary men, many of the scientists, besides the innumerable unclassified, and within a year was elected a member of the St. James's Club. He was, on the whole, he admits, treated better than in Washington. By another three years he notes that "as though to make him more helpless and wholly to distort his life, England grew more and more agreeable and amusing." When the time came for leaving, his heart was wrenched. "He loved his haunts, his houses, his habits, even his hansom cabs. He loved growling like an Englishman, and going into society where he knew not a face, and cared not a straw." When he returned to London from America in 1870 he tells us how he sniffed "with voluptuous delight the coalsmoke of Cheapside" and then, with an unusual burst of emotion, he exclaims "he loved it all—everything—had always loved it!" The education he had received was immense, and we must duly consider such passages as the above when we hear him "growling like an Englishman" and denouncing their national stupidity.

His diplomatic training had been unique. We need not here enumerate the successive crises which the cool, balanced judgment of his father so successfully surmounted. We need merely note that probably in the entire history of the United States no diplomatic post has been of importance equal to that held by the elder Adams from 1861 to 1868. During the whole of it, Henry was his father's confidant, watching the finespun webs from the very center and sharing his father's keen intellectual analysis of situation after situation, menacing the position of the North and threatening the passing of our Civil War into a world conflagration.

Meanwhile, that war went on. Most of Henry's friends, including his brother Charles, were in the army, and Henry, in 1861, in an outburst against the supposed disagreeableness of his position in London and with the sedentary's sense of frustration when faced with a world of intense action, had threatened to go into the army himself. It might have been a good thing if he had, unsuited as he was physically, but the mood passed easily under fraternal dissuadings and a feeling of duty toward his father. At the center of diplomacy and in contact with the much greater strength of his father's character, the vision of power again possessed the younger man. "One began," he wrote, "to dream the sensation of wielding unmeasured power. The sense came, like vertigo, for an instant, and passed, leaving the brain a little dazed, doubtful, shy." In this essay there is no claim made to present the "true" Henry Adams. Who can be sure that he

knows all the secret springs of character and con-
duct even in those nearest to him in life? When
one has to delineate a human soul from fragmentary
documents, it is merely insolent egotism to claim
that one has infallibly plumbed the depths. The
main preoccupation of both Henry and his father
for many years was to reach the motives of Russell
and Palmerston, yet neither was ever sure that he
did, so difficult is human nature even when in actual
contact. I may, therefore, be quite wrong, but
from living with the writings of Adams I carry the
impression that the key to much of his life and attitude lies in the sentences I have just quoted. The
dream of power was always, until it was too late,
recurring to him, but he was always a little "dazed,
doubtful, shy."

Unfitted by the whole of his heritage and by
temperament for the struggle for power in the open
arena of either business or politics, as they were
conducted in the late nineteenth century, there was
no road left but an appointive office, say, the Secretary of State or an Ambassadorship, *faute de mieux,*

or the wielding of power through the press. That
he would have made a good diplomatist is, I think,
highly questionable. That he had an acute and
subtle mind is true but, as he never tires of telling
us, he was of the eighteenth century. He would
have felt at home at the Congress of Vienna. The
mass-mind, however, was beginning to loom more
and more portentous among social forces, and the
mass-mind always remained both uninteresting and
unintelligible to Adams. Nor, with all his years
of residence abroad, is it clear that the foreign mind
ever became wholly understandable to him. One
must not expect too much of the young amateur
diplomatist in London from the age of twenty-three
to thirty, although his training should have made
him far more mature than most young diplomatists
of that age, and his opportunities for enlightenment
were unusual. During those years the chief antagonists in the drama were Palmerston and Russell,
yet analyzing them afresh after forty years, in the
light of subsequently published documents, he admitted that "they made a picture different from

anything he had conceived and rendered worthless his whole diplomatic experience." He adds, with an echo of his comment on the University of Berlin, that "the American type was more familiar."

If he did not reach the minds of his father's chief antagonists, neither did he display the understanding of the general diplomatic situation in 1861 which not only his father did but also his brother, though the latter was in the army three thousand miles away. Henry became insanely convinced that England intended to force us into declaring war against herself. When, in the absence of his father on a country house visit, the news reached the Legation of the capture of Mason and Slidell, not only the Legation secretaries but also Henry "broke into shouts of delight. They were glad to face the end. They saw it and cheered it!" The sober words of both father and brother in their letters throw into rather lurid contrast the utterly wrong track on which the mind of Henry was galloping headlong.[1]

[1] *A Cycle of Adams Letters,* ed. W. C. Ford, Boston, 1920, vol. I, pp. 79-82.

Nor do Henry's literary activities at this time throw his diplomatic abilities into any better light. Unknown to his father, he was writing a series of letters which were being published in the *New York Times*. Not only was Adams convinced that England "means to make war," but he was attempting to brandish that firebrand irresponsibly in an American journal. His egotism and lack of balance are clearly shown in a letter of his of December 13, 1861. The American people, he writes to his brother, are "a bloody set of fools" because they do not agree with Henry that England wants war and will have it over the Mason-Slidell capture. "You're mad, all of you. It's pitiable to see such idiocy in a nation. There's the *New York Times* which I warned only in my last letter against such an act, and its consequences; and now I find the passage erased, and editorial assurances that war was *impossible* on such grounds. Egad, who knew best, Raymond [1] or I? War is not only possible but inevitable." The letters, of course, were un-

[1] The editor of the *Times*.

signed but one hesitates over what to wonder at most, the colossal egotism of a young man holding his own opinion against a world of "bloody fools" or the sight of the son of a Minister writing to the newspapers that the country to which his father is accredited intends war against his own.

The young man, however, was soon to get a fright over his undiplomatic proceedings. He had written, at the suggestion of his brother, an article on the Cotton Famine in England which his brother had published in the *Boston Courier*. Henry's signature was not appended but the article was attributed to him in a brief note in the editorial column. It was immediately discovered by the London *Times* which devoted to it, January 10, 1862, a satirical leading article, to the complete confusion of Henry. He thought for the moment that his "usefulness" was over. Luckily, for once in a way, he discovered the value of obscurity. A careful study of the *Education* shows that Adams wrote it from memory unrefreshed by turning to contemporary documents. He says that "luckily the *Times* did not know its victim to be a part, though not an official, of the Legation, and lost the chance to make the satire fatal." As a matter of fact, reference to the *Times* reveals that it began its article by saying that "Mr. H. Adams, son of the American 'Minister in London,' seems to have been deputed, in November last, to report on the feelings of Manchester toward the Federal States," and indulges in no light raillery at the social experiences in London of the son of the "American Minister." As the *Times* thus not only knew but openly proclaimed that its article was directed at the son of the Minister and that he was living in London, it is difficult to understand, in view of the fact that Adams had no official connection with the Legation, what more Joe Parkes could have told its editors, as described in the *Education*.

Although in his memoirs, Adams made light of the affair, he was at the moment thoroughly frightened, and the morning that the *Times* publicly ridiculed him he wrote in a panic to his brother that he was being "laughed at by all England." He discovered in a lightning flash that a diplomat's son might display more zeal than discretion. His father, he wrote to his brother, bore the vexation very good-naturedly but "another would be my ruin for a long time." His father knew nothing of the correspondence Henry was so assiduously printing in the *New York Times*. "I don't want him ever to know about it," wrote the scared young diplomat. He did not even dare to write to Raymond to explain why he would never write any more, for fear his letter should get out. He begged his brother to do the job for him as "my connection with him must on no account be known." For the rest of his father's term he "wrote no more letters, and meddled with no more newspapers." Thereafter he devoted himself to "escorting American ladies to drawing-rooms, or American gentlemen to levees at St. James's Palace, or bowing solemnly to people with great titles, at Court balls, or even awkwardly jostling royalty at garden parties," for all of which, he wrote, "neither President Lincoln nor Secretary Seward would ever know enough of their business to thank him for doing what they did not know how to get properly done by their own servants."

IN SEARCH OF A CAREER

5.

IN SEARCH OF A CAREER

THE Civil War at length came to an end, but
Minister Adams was retained at London. It
was obvious, however, that he could not remain
there forever, and his son began again his quest for a
career. His father, he says, agreed with him that
two careers were closed. "For the law, diplomacy
had unfitted him; for diplomacy he already knew
too much." Henry was, at the time (it was 1866),
twenty-eight years of age, no older than thousands
of other young men who, after serving five years
in the army, were likewise looking about them to
patch together broken educations or interrupted
ambitions. One cannot but think that the heavy
weight of his heritage made itself felt at this point

upon his hesitating and timorous temper. His
grandfather, John Quincy, of sterner stuff, after
being abroad seven years and serving as private
secretary to the American Minister at St. Petersburg and to his father during the peace negotiations with England, asserted his character and,
declining further private service to his father as
Minister to England, returned to graduate from
Harvard, spend dull years in a law office and to
be admitted to the bar when thirty-three. Had it
not been for Henry's heritage, there is no reason
why five years spent in war-service as a private secretary in London, though, like the army, it might
make a transition to a law office unpalatable for a
while, should have made it impossible for him.

At twenty he had toyed with the idea of becoming a lawyer and emigrating to St. Louis, but Mr.
Dana had treated this idea "with a little contempt,"
and that, apparently, was sufficient to dissuade the
not over-enthusiastic young emigrant. Dana "insisted," wrote Henry to his brother, "that I was
looking toward politics; and perhaps he was right.

There are two things that seem to be at the bottom of our constitutions; one is a continual tendency towards politics; the other is family pride; and it is strange how these two feelings run through all of us." [1] He adds that, for himself he had set politics aside and was looking then only to the law. That, however, had been seven years earlier and before Henry had watched his father wield power in London.

One feels that the crux of the difficulty was to find any career that would lead in a dignified way to anything sufficiently big for a fourth generation Adams. Had Henry's ancestors been ordinary upper-class Americans and had he been acting as private secretary to a stranger instead of to his father, he would have merely thanked his lucky stars for an interesting experience and got down to work, precisely as after any war temporary brigadier-generals slip back to captaincies in the hope of making their way up again, and others in high places start afresh, the better for the education

[1] *Letters,* cit supra, p. 5.

and the more ambitious for their day of power. In Henry's case, however, the weight of accumulated safeguards which had pressed on the cradle in Hancock Avenue continued to press on the young man riding his hack in Rotten Row. "One profession alone seemed possible—the press."

"For the press, then, Henry Adams," he writes, "decided to fit himself, and since he could not go home to get practical training, he set himself to work to do what he could in London," though he knew, he adds, that it was not the way to do it. Why he thought he could not go home is a conundrum. When he had wanted for a moment to enter the army, he had threatened to abandon his father at the beginning of his term in a thoroughly hostile environment. He had later decided that it was his duty to remain and be on hand, which was entirely reasonable. But by 1866 his father had become an institution in London society. He had attained an unique rank there, which even the *Times* conceded. "The years of struggle were over," his son wrote, "and Minister Adams rapidly gained a position which would have caused his father or grandfather to stare with incredulous envy." The British never did things by halves and the Minister had become a "kind of American peer of the Realm." He was only fifty-nine years old and was to live for another quarter of a century. Had his twenty-eight-year-old son moved to go home and begin his own career, the father would have made no objection. The fact seems to be that in spite of his jibes at British stupidity and other unendearing qualities, Henry found life in London exceedingly agreeable and tearing one's self away from it no easy matter. In 1864 some of his family having suffered from the English climate, he had been detailed to escort them to Italy, where he spent six months. "Travelling," he notes, "in all possible luxury, at some one else's expense, with diplomatic privileges and position, was a form of travel hitherto untried," and he quite naturally enjoyed it hugely. London life as the son of the Minister was becoming a habit, though "as often as he could, Adams ran over to Paris, for sunshine and there always sought out Richardson . . . and they went off to dine at the Palais Royal, and talk of whatever interested the students of the Beaux Arts." In 1863 he had written to his brother of that "young Europe, of which I am by tastes and education a part." In spite of his Americanism and his constant irony he was to become more and more a part of it in a way that none of his ancestors had done. Taking all together, it is not hard to see why, an American newspaper career determined upon, he lingered another two years until his father himself resigned and returned to Boston.

Henry, however, was no idling dilettante. Quite apart from the invaluable aids to his education that the social contacts, with which his father's position provided him, afforded, he had worked hard. Like all his ancestors since the portraits began, he possessed intellectual curiosity in the best French sense, was a voracious reader, and had for long periods at a time the scholar's willingness to suffer drudgery. "I am ruining my constitution," he wrote his brother, "by studying far into the small hours," or again, "my candles are seldom out before two o'clock in the morning, and my table is spoiled with half-read books and unfinished writing. For weeks together I only leave the house to mount my horse and after my ride come back as I went." He studied De Tocqueville, Mill and Comte, and began his later marked interest in science with Darwin and Lyell. He had seen and learned much more and worked much harder than the over-done irony of the *Education* would indicate. Both by experience and study few young men of twenty-eight could then have had as good equipment for the rôle of publicist as Adams had. It was the rôle he was now to essay to play.

It has been said that he never craved public office. It has even been said that he would not have accepted it had it been offered to him. The second statement obviously can be positively asserted of no one. To assert it of Adams I think absurd. For a century his family had been the recipients of the highest offices to which the nation could appoint them. Had he been offered at some stage of his life the ambassadorship to England it is incredible that both inherited instinct and a sense of duty would have allowed him to decline. Indeed, he has himself said that "there never was a day when he would have refused any duty that the government imposed upon him" or to accept any office. "But," he added, "no President had ever invited him to fill one." As he grew older, he may well have preferred his own life as it was to a public one but I do not think that was true of his younger days. He was unfitted both by weight of heritage and by his own qualities and lack of others for the rough-and-tumble scramble for power which marked most careers open to him in the late nineteenth century. Nevertheless, there would seem to be no doubt, if we may take his own words as guide, that he embarked upon his career as a writer in the hope that it would lead in some form to that power which he has said all the young generation of his family, like their fathers before them, had craved.

During the next few years, he had his eye on the

New York press, and what he was aiming at was power, possibly as mere publicist, possibly as editor of a New York daily. The first start he made was, indeed, an essay in American antiquarianism, the essay on "Captain John Smith" which was published in the *North American Review*. Palfrey had suggested it to "Adams, who wanted to make a position for himself" as "likely to break as much glass, as any other stone that could be thrown by a beginner." If the object rather than the nature of the essay is interesting as evidence of Adams's ambition, that is also true of his next one. One day Sir Charles Lyell dropped in at the Legation for advice as to how to get his *Principles of Geology* noticed in America. Adams suggested that he himself review it, and the offer was accepted. Two other articles followed, those on "British Finance in 1816" and "The Bank of England Restriction, 1797-1821," and all were accepted by the *North American Review*. Of that journal Adams says significantly that "it was an organ worth playing on; and, in the fancy of Henry Adams, it led, in some indistinct future, to playing on a New York daily newspaper." To anticipate a little, we may also note that when writing for the press from Washington in 1869 he says he had "his eye, not on the government, but on New York," and the next year when he was being persuaded to accept the editorship of the *Review* and the position at Harvard he was urged on the score that it would lead to the daily press. In writing the "Session" in 1869 he says it was with the intention of gradually establishing himself as a political authority and making the newspapers reckon with him as a power "more effective than all the speeches in Congress or reports to the President, that could be crammed into the government presses." This, then, appears to have been his ambition when around thirty years of age. He would accept office on the condition that it was offered to him and that he should not strive for it. In the absence of that he would attempt to control power from the quiet of his study.

It is true that at times he stated his aim differ-

HENRY ADAMS, AT THE AGE OF THIRTY

From a Sketch made by Samuel Lawrence in 1868

ently. In a rather remarkable comment upon himself in 1870 he says of his writing that "if he worked at all, it was for social consideration, and social pleasure was his pay. Artists have done it from the beginning of time, and will do it after time has expired, since they cannot help themselves, and they find their return in the pride of their social superiority as they feel it. Society commonly abets them and encourages their attitude of contempt." This amazing dictum that the mainspring of an artist's activity is snobbishness is perhaps mainly interesting as throwing light from an unexpected angle upon Adams's own lack of deep æsthetic emotions and satisfactions. It does not alter the probability that his own ambition was for power in some form, though from dreams of political power he may have descended to the lower level of playing for social consideration. His brother, Brooks, indeed once said that Henry had achieved what he really wanted most, though he may not always have known it, and that that was social consideration and distinction.

In connection with these several points, it is interesting to note the reasons which he gave to his pupil, Henry Cabot Lodge, a few years later when suggesting that that young man, then also in search of a career, should become a historian. Adams pointed out that no one had made more money in business than Motley, Parkman or Bancroft had as historians; that a successful history would enable Lodge to set himself up in Boston "as a species of literary lion with ease"; and that with that position would come "social dignity, European reputation, *and a foreign mission to close.*" [1] One cannot but wonder which of these reasons for becoming a historian may have been uppermost in Adams's mind when he himself later became one for several laborious years.

It is a rare man who does not at different times and in different moods want different things, and who through life keeps his ambition in a single line. Henry was not of that type. He changed, I think, greatly as he grew older. To consider that

[1] *Letters,* cit supra, p. 228. Italics mine.

the author of the *Mont-Saint-Michel and Chartres*
and the *Education,* declining to publish them, was
working for power, either political or social, is absurd, but the Henry of 1900 was not the Henry
of 1870. In the work done by the earlier Henry,
unless we must consider as false everything he has
himself said, he was clearly thinking not of the
work but of what it would bring him in some form
of power. He worked neither as artist, scholar
nor seeker for truth but as a man who wielded
his pen for the sake of his ambition in other fields,
though the ambition gave but a flickering light and
an inconstant heat. Of himself he had written to his
brother in 1862, "I am convinced that a man whose
mind is balanced like mine, in such a way that
what is evil never seems unmixed with good, and
what is good always streaked with evil; an object
never important enough to call out strong energies
till they are exhausted, nor necessary enough not
to allow of its failure being possible to retrieve, in
short, a mind which is not strongly positive and
absolute, cannot be steadily successful in action,

which requires quietness and perseverance." It was the mind of Henry Adams but it was not the mind of a great leader of public opinion as editor of the daily press. Nevertheless, Adams set himself to work.

In his writings in London in 1867 he had tried three different fields, history, economics and science, with the mere hope of bringing himself before the public. The "John Smith" had been written "to break glass" and "make a position for himself" rather than as the stone in a historical edifice. The bid for practical power in a practical world was also made in the two articles on finance, always Adams's weakest subject. The appeal was made not to scholars but to those in power. The currency question and resumption of payments being burning ones in the United States after the war, Adams "thought he might win a name among financiers and statesmen at home by showing how this task had been done in England after the classical suspension of 1797-1821." For the two years after his return to America this was to be his dominant motive.

THE JOURNALIST

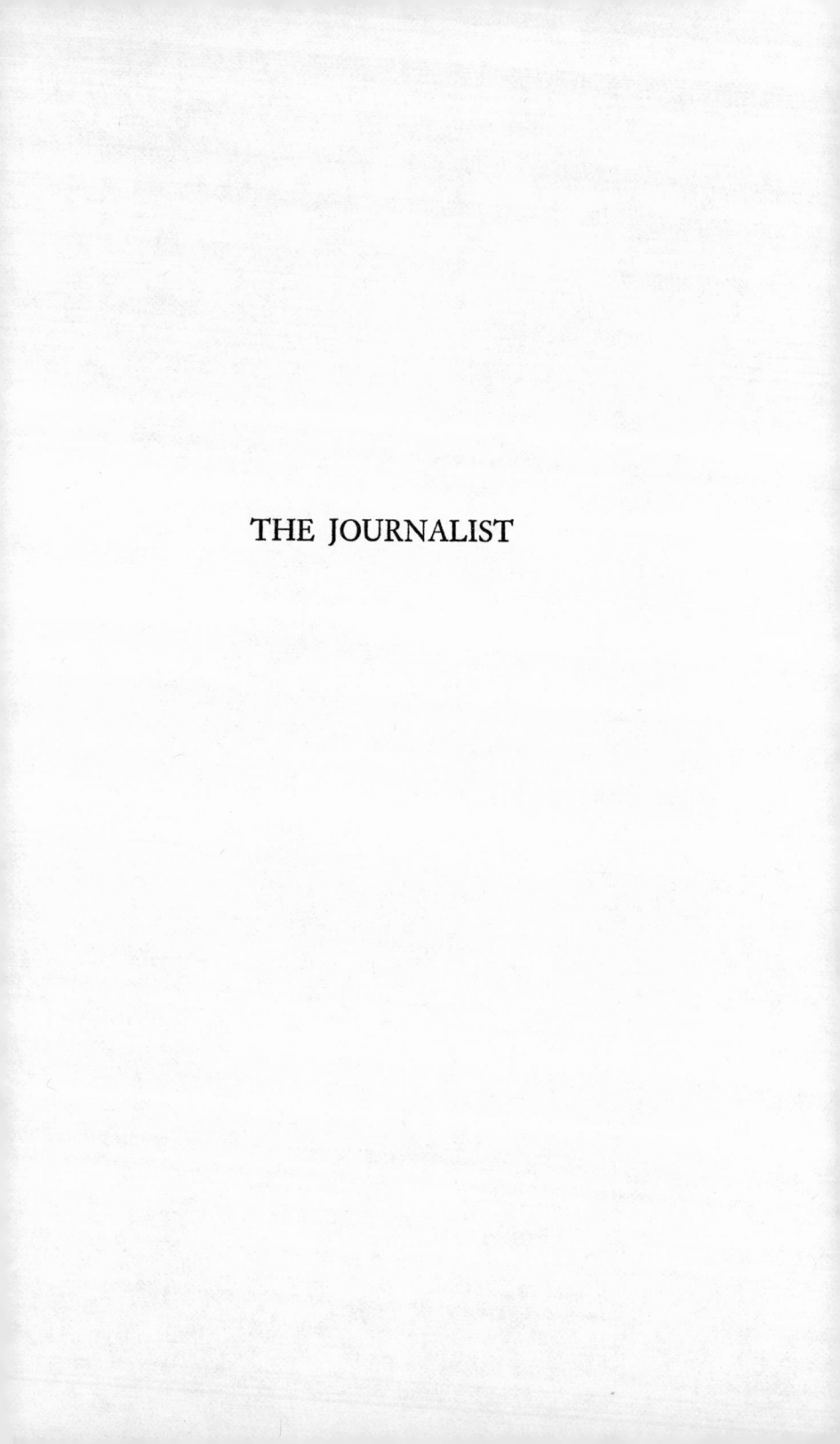

6.

THE JOURNALIST

THE Adamses returned with John Lothrop Motley and his family in July, 1868, landing at New York. Fresh from the ordered civilization of London Henry was plunged into a seething population of all races bent solely on creating the tools of a new economic order—"capital, banks, mines, furnaces, shops, power-houses, technical knowledge, mechanical population, together with a steady remodelling of social and political habits, ideas and institutions to fit the new scale and suit the new conditions." "The new Americans, of whom he was to be one, must, whether they were fit or unfit, create a world of their own, a science, a society, a philosophy, a universe, where they had not yet created a road or even learned to dig their own iron. They had no time for thought; they saw, and could see, nothing beyond their day's work; their attitude to the universe outside them was that of the deep-sea fish. Above all, they naturally and intensely disliked to be told what to do, and how to do it, by men who took their ideas and their methods from the abstract theories of history, philosophy, or theology. They knew enough to know that their world was one of energies quite new." Adams found himself at sea, ejected from his own heritage as the Indians and the buffalo had been ejected from theirs. "He vehemently insisted that he was not himself at fault. The defeat was not due to him, nor yet to any superiority of his rivals. He had been unfairly forced out of the track, and must get back into it as best he could." His brother, John Quincy the younger, had gone into politics "on the wrong side." Charles, foreseeing the prime importance of railroads, had gone in for them. Henry, back in Quincy and Boston, spent some months visiting relatives, looking over the situation, and then reaffirmed his decision to strike for the press, he and Charles hoping to play into each other's hands in striving for power under the conditions of the new America.

Adams had never felt himself at home in Boston. Even as a boy, he writes, that "he felt himself shut out of Boston as though he were an exile; he never thought of himself as a Bostonian. . . . Always he felt himself somewhere else; perhaps in Washington with its social ease; perhaps in Europe; and he watched with vague unrest from the Quincy hills the smoke of the Cunard steamers stretching in a long line to the horizon . . . as though the steamers were offering to take him away." On his return now he found himself still more unfitted for the life of the city where he had been born. "No one trusted his temperament or education; he had to go." He says elsewhere that he was wrong in his opinion of the city, that "the thinness was in himself, not in Boston" but the feeling was there. Either his father had changed his opinion or Adams's recollections are at fault, for he says of this period that the father would have been glad to keep his son at home and have him again take up the study of law. The young man decided, however, for Washington and the press, and to that city he went, in the travelling company of William M. Evarts, in October, 1868.

Evarts at once took Adams to the White House and introduced him to President Johnson, who "was not the sort of man whom a young reformer of thirty, with two or three foreign educations, was likely to see with enthusiasm," although Adams later admitted that Johnson was perhaps the strongest executive as a President whom he had ever seen. Washington in those days was a "happy village." "In four-and-twenty hours," Adams says, "he could know everybody; in two days everybody knew him." There was no club. A single express train came and went daily to the outer world. The one-horse tram on F Street provided amply for all the city's traffic. The country began at Lafayette Square. After London, "the Washington world offered an easy and delightful repose." Adams lived with Mr. Evarts, then Attorney-General. Life was amusing, even having to "learn to talk to Western Congressmen, and to hide his own antecedents." He could count on the *North American Review* for his heavier articles, and on the *Nation* for correspondence. He had more difficulty, however, with what he wanted most, a New York daily. Raymond of the *Times* had died. For personal and political reasons he considered the *Tribune* out of the question. Adams, because "with the best intentions he must always fail as a blackguard," felt that he could not please Dana of the *Sun* and himself at the same time. The *Herald* admitted no personality but that of Bennett. There was nothing left but the "free-trade Holy Land of the *Evening Post* under William Cullen Bryant, while beside it lay only the elevated plateau of the New Jerusalem occupied by Godkin and the *Nation*," in both of which he reached only the readers of the *North American*.

Although he did not consider the outlook very hopeful, he set to work. The *Nation* published correspondence and Adams planned such longer articles as he thought would do the most good. He worked for three months on the subject of the American finances, and sent the article, "American Finance, 1865-1869," to his friend Henry Reeve, editor of the *Edinburgh Review,* who published it in April, 1869. Like all such contributions in the English reviews of that day, publication was anonymous, but Adams says he was not asking for advertisement in connection with it but for help in establishing his literary rank and in the hope of winning a permanent place on the staff of the *Edinburgh* under the shadow of Lord Macaulay. The English might be "stupid," but such rank then seemed to Adams the highest in the literary world. Although the article would thus not bring his name immediately before the American public, it was reprinted in America, and was a well-considered step in his plan for a career.

This finished, he turned to a scheme he had in mind for the *North American.* Lord Robert Cecil, later Lord Salisbury, in England had invented an annual review of politics which he called "The Session" and published through the *Quarterly*. Adams seized on the idea and "began what he meant for a permanent series of annual political reviews which he hoped to make, in time, a political authority." Here he had the field to himself, and with the advantage of the friendships he possessed in Washington he intended to make his publication an organ of power, which, as we have noted above, he thought might be more effective than all the speeches of Congress. Part One of "The Session" was printed in the *North American* in April, 1869; another portion, too long to be included in the first part, was printed with the separate title of "Civil Service Reform" in October; and "The Session," Part II, in July, 1870. Yet another, "The Legal-Tender Act," which he had written in collaboration with Francis A. Walker, was published in April. Meanwhile Grant had entered the White House, and Jay Gould and Jim Fisk had nearly wrecked the country with their operations in the Gold Market in New York. The great scandal and mystery of the day were the problem of Gould's connection with Grant in his operations. Charles and Henry Adams jumped at the chance to unravel it. Leaving the story of Gould and his railways to Charles, Henry undertook to work out that of the Gold Conspiracy. He finished it by early spring, considering it the best piece of work he had yet done, and determined to publish it in England, as London was a good place to strike at Gould. An article in an English review attracted much more attention than in an American one.

So far, everything connected with his writing had gone as well as Adams could possibly have hoped. He had found Washington excessively amusing and "never had been so busy, so interested, so much in the thick of the crowd. He knew Congressmen by scores, and newspaper-men by the dozen. He wrote for his various organs all sorts of attacks and defences. He enjoyed the life immensely"; but soon he suddenly abandoned it.

Whether he intended to do so before he sailed for England in the spring of 1870 is not certain, for one cannot count too much on the exact order in which impressions, ideas and comments occur in the *Education*. In that volume, before speaking of the English expedition, Adams notes that the second part of the "Session," that of 1869-1870, was his last study in contemporary politics. In one place he speaks of the latter year as marking the end of a literary epoch, "when quarterlies gave way to monthlies; letter press to illustration; volumes to pages." He might, however, have adjusted himself to new vehicles of expression, for, after all, he had been steadily aiming at the daily press. What gave the blow to his hopes and ambitions was the character of the administration of Grant, for whom Adams himself had voted. America, as he says, reverted to the stone-age. The publication of the names of the new President's cabinet was enough. "After such a miscarriage," wrote Adams, "no thought of effectual reform could revive for at least one generation, and he [Adams] had no fancy for ineffectual politics. What course could he sail next? He had tried so many, and society had barred them all!" For the moment he decided to continue as he was. He felt, however, that he was through. Speaking of the "Session of 1869-1870," he says that "he could have said no more, had he gone on reviewing every session in the rest of the century. The political dilemma was as clear in 1870 as it was likely to be in 1970. The system of 1789 had broken down, and with it the eighteenth-century fabric of *a priori,* or moral, principles."

At any rate, "he needed to get back to London for the season," and by May he was once again driving down St. James's Street. He had taken the manuscript of "The Gold Conspiracy" with him intending it for Reeve and the *Edinburgh Review.* To his amazement, Reeve proved fearful of libel and refused it, as did also the editor of the *Quarterly.* It subsequently found lodgement in the pages of the *Westminster* to which Adams had dispatched it when called suddenly to Italy where his sister was dying of tetanus after a carriage accident.

For the first time, perhaps, in his life, Adams

felt the searing flame of a primitive emotion, which even his habitual reticence does not conceal in the pages of the *Education*. Slowly he revived from "the distorted nightmare of his personal horror" and made his way back to the peace of Wenlock Abbey and his friend Milnes Gaskell in England. There by mail he received an offer from President Eliot to Harvard to become an Assistant Professor of History in a chair soon to be created. He declined, and sailed for home in a despondent mood. "The summer, from which he had expected only amusement and social relations with new people, had ended in the most intimate personal tragedy, and the most terrific political convulsion [the Franco-Prussian War] he had ever known or was likely to know. He had failed in every object of his trip. The Quarterlies had refused his best essay. He had made no acquaintances and hardly picked up the old ones. He sailed from Liverpool, on September 1, to begin again where he had started two years before, but with no longer a hope of attaching himself to a President or a party or a press. He was a free lance and no other career stood in sight or mind."

Once home, things looked brighter. He says in the *Education* that the second part of his Session article had been reprinted in hundreds of thousands of copies as a campaign document, but this is evidently another slip of unrefreshed memory, and the reasoning based on it fails to hold. The article was not thus published until two years later and could therefore have been of no encouragement to him at this time. Of his two recalled successes, which in memory made him wish to continue his journalistic career, one thus fails him in the light of contemporary evidence, and makes his family action less bludgeoning than Adams pictures it.

At any rate, he did receive news of the acceptance of his "Gold Conspiracy," and the article was pirated in American journals on a colossal scale. He suggests that in spite of Grant and society, he wanted to go back to Washington but that his family interfered. "No sooner had Adams made at Washington what he modestly hoped was a sufficient success, than his whole family set on him to drag him away. For the first time since 1861 his father interposed; his mother entreated; and his brother Charles argued and urged that he should come to Harvard College. Charles had views of further joint operations in a new field. He said Henry had done at Washington all he could possibly do; that his position there wanted solidity; that he was, after all, an adventurer; that a few years in Cambridge would give him personal weight; that his chief function was not to be that of teacher, but that of editing the *North American Review* which was to be coupled with the professorship, and would lead to the daily press."

THE PROFESSOR

7.

THE PROFESSOR

ADAMS had great respect for his brother-in-law Professor Gurney, who was head of the history department, and who urged the double post upon him. Henry felt that the others had the right to guide him, and that after all, "it could not much affect the sum of solar energies whether one went on dancing with girls in Washington, or began talking to boys at Cambridge." He saw Eliot and protested that he knew nothing of medieval history. Eliot suggested that Adams name anyone who knew more. Adams could not, accepted the posts, and, with his brother Brooks, at once settled in rooms in the old house of his aunt, Mrs. Edward Everett. For the next nine months he tells us, he exhausted his energy and consumed all his time in keeping one day ahead of his class.

His advisers were justified and the step was probably one of the wisest Adams had ever taken. He himself described this period of his life in a chapter of the *Education* called "Failure" but it was far from being so. One of his scholars has written more fairly of it than he would himself.[1] At that time the graduate school did not yet exist and Adams introduced the first real seminar and research method into American universities. The few graduate students Adams had were in the habit of dining more or less with him in the house at 91 Marlboro Street, which he afterwards took, and held their meetings in his library before the open fire. They delved deep into the legal codes of the Visigoths, Burgundians and Salian Franks, each being left very much to himself in his researches. Laughlin says that besides the writings of numerous German authorities, they read many times the whole

[1] J. Laurence Laughlin, "Some Recollections of Henry Adams," *Scribner's Magazine*, May, 1921.

collection of Anglo-Saxon laws "and ploughed through twenty-five thousand pages of charters and capitularies in mediæval Latin." "Throughout all this adventure in research Adams was like a colt in tall clover. He was fattening himself for his next move on English constitutional history on the way to his important work on the 'History of the United States.' " We may note here, somewhat out of chronological order, that several of the doctorates of the young men submitted for the degree of Ph.D. were published in 1876 in a volume entitled *Essays in Anglo-Saxon Law,* to which Adams himself contributed the first essay, "The Anglo-Saxon Courts of Law."

In contact with his students, Adams must have been immensely stimulating with his originality of thought, his unexpected remarks and even his explosive manner. Laughlin reports that one day when Adams was asked just what *transubstantiation* meant, he answered "Good Heavens! How should I know! Look it up!" and that Adams was the first man who awoke in him a love of learning. To Laughlin, Adams's mind revealed itself as virile and robust rather than subtle, displaying an incessant intellectual curiosity. Too many facts, however, bored him, and he preferred imaginative guesses. Already the student noted that Adams had an *a priori* assumption that history was evolutionary and should be found to follow certain laws. In 1915, Adams wrote to his old pupil, Henry Osborn Taylor, saying, "I never loved or taught facts, if I could help it, having that antipathy to facts which only idiots and philosophers attain," [1] and Dr. Taylor recalls him as saying in one of his classes that "for facts as such I have a profound contempt." At first Adams had set his boys to work on Hallam's *Middle Ages* and Duruy's *Histoire du Moyen Age,* but later, by the time three instructors had been added to the department, he was giving lectures on the constitutional and legal history of England down to the seventeenth century. In 1875-1876 he gave a course in American Colonial

[1] Mss. letter, Henry Adams to Henry Osborn Taylor, Feb. 15, 1915.

History, and in the following year one on American
Constitutional Government. Dr. Taylor took these
courses in his Sophomore and Junior years, and
writes me, of his first meeting with Adams, that
he remembers "going to an upper room in University building, and seeing the room rather full,
and a small disgusted looking man sitting at the
desk. He took a look around at the students, and
then delivered a screed on the difficulty of his pro-
posed course, which frightened away a good half—
as he intended." Adams frequently set subjects for
debate between two of his students, and on one occasion Taylor and A. Lawrence Lowell, another
student, were set to debating the constitutionality
of the Act of Congress creating the Bank of the
United States. There were no text books used in
either of these two American history courses (the
only ones Adams ever gave), the students being sent
direct to the sources. As an indication of the effect
Adams had on his students we may quote an entry
in the diary of the young Henry Osborn Taylor,
himself to become in later years one of the great-

est of American historical scholars. In the beginning of his Junior year, October 1, 1876, the boy,
after listing his courses and professors, noted that
"Adams I think I like more than any other instruc-
tor; he is so clear-headed and analyzed history so
well; also he despises, as I do, the barren accumu-
lation of knowledge and also dilettantism." [1]

During this period of his life as teacher and editor, Adams himself wrote almost nothing. A few
of his essays were reprinted in 1871 in the volume
Chapters of Erie and Other Essays, and one article,
"Harvard College, 1786-1787" had appeared in
the *North American.* Also from this period there
is the essay on Anglo-Saxon Law already noted;
one on "The Primitive Rights of Women," given
as a Lowell Institute Lecture but not printed until
1891; and a number of book reviews in the *North
American.* Adams professed to find these years,
1870-1877, so far as his work was concerned, the
most barren of his life. Of all educations, he says,
he found that of school-teacher the thinnest, though

[1] Letter from H. O. Taylor to the author, June 17, 1929.

that of editor was in some ways thinner still. Editorial success, he found, lay in getting advertisements,—ten pages spelling success and five failure. As he had already noted, the days of the Quarterlies were passing, but in spite of his own opinion, Adams managed to maintain the high standard of his journal and not infrequently was able to print important and lasting articles. The work, however, bored him, and kept him wholly from original writing himself. In Harvard, he enjoyed his students but found lecturing futile and faculty meetings worse. Socially he preferred even Congressmen to professors, and found Cambridge "a social desert that would have starved a polar bear" in spite of the presence of "some of the liveliest and most agreeable of men—James Russell Lowell, Francis J. Child, Louis Agassiz, his son, Alexander, Gurney, John Fiske, William James and a dozen others, who would have made the joy of London or Paris" had not society spoiled them by dubbing them professor.

The seven years spent there, however, whatever

they may have seemed to Adams, did much for him. While he was in London, his brother Charles had written to him that "all a man's life is not meant for books, or for travel in Europe," and had urged him to do anything that called for hardship,—even a trip to the North Pole,—without which he would never be a man. In 1870 Henry was a brilliant but a somewhat irritating boy. By 1877 we find him, Henry Adams indeed still, but solidified with no loss of brilliancy. As professor at Harvard he had had not only an established position for seven years, due to his own efforts and not to his ancestry, but he had left his mark permanently on the educational system of his country. As editor of the *Review* he had had a training in just that responsibility and routine which he needed. Ironically as he chose to treat both episodes, he could not but know that he had done well, and that the Adams of 1877 was much more of a man than the discontented ex-private secretary to his father of 1870.

Two more personal happenings during these

CLARENCE KING

years had their influence also. In 1871 he had taken a trip through the Colorado mountains and beyond, then really frontier, on which by accident he met Clarence King, "coming from the West, saturated with the sunshine of the Sierras." King was thenceforth to be his closest friend. The hunting, fishing, and roughing it undoubtedly did Adams a world of good, as did the new friendship with a man who had all Adams dreamed of as education and yet who spent his life in the open instead of in drawing rooms, libraries and galleries. The following year, 1872, was marked by Adams's marriage on June 27th, to Marian Hooper, the daughter of Doctor Robert William Hooper, a distinguished physician and surgeon, of Boston. Doctor Hooper had married Ellen Sturgis, so that Adams's wife was a granddaughter, on one side, of John Hooper, a wealthy and influential bank president of Marblehead, and, on the other, of William Sturgis, a wealthy Boston merchant. Adams's later career was made possible, or at least greatly facilitated, by the moderate wealth which thus came to him by marriage.

Women always loomed large in Adams's mind as a possible cultural influence, but his experience of them in that rôle appears to have been comparatively limited until his marriage. Of his youthful years in Boston he wrote that every youngster was always falling in love from the age of seven with some girl "who had nothing to teach him, or he to teach her, except rather familiar and provincial manners, until they married and bore children to repeat the habit. The idea of attaching one's self to a married woman, or of polishing one's manners to suit the standards of a woman of thirty, could hardly have entered the mind of a young Bostonian, and would have scandalized his parents. From women the boy got the domestic virtues and nothing else. He might not even catch the idea that women had more to give. The Garden of Eden was hardly more primitive." In his account of his first two years of Europe he scarcely mentions a woman other than a landlady and the "usual plain daughters" of a landlord, except his sister. Of her he wrote, speaking of himself at twenty-one, that "she was the first young woman he was ever intimate with—quick, sensitive, wilful, or full of will, energetic, sympathetic and intelligent enough to supply a score of men with ideas—and he was delighted to give her the reins—to let her drive him where she would. It was his first experiment in giving the reins to a woman, and he was so much pleased with the results that he never wanted to take them back. In after life he made a general law of experience— no woman had ever driven him wrong; no man had ever driven him right." We have already noted her tragic death in 1870, an event of both deep emotional and intellectual influence upon Adams.

During his seven years at the Legation in London he appears to have had few intimate social relations with women, Mrs. Russell Sturgis being an exception. There was, indeed, the extraordinary Lady Palmerston whom foreigners called *sympathique* and who maintained the best political house in town but contrived to do so with apparently "no effort beyond a friendly recognition." He speaks of the "compliment and the pleasure" derived from the friendship offered him by the mother and aunt of his friend Milnes Gaskell but notes otherwise that "English women, from the educational point of view, could give nothing until they approached forty years old. Then they became very interesting—very charming—to the man of fifty. The young American was not worth the young Englishwoman's notice, and never received it. Neither understood the other. Only in domestic relation, in the country—never in society at large—a young American might accidentally make friends with an Englishwoman of his own age, but it never happened to Henry Adams. His susceptible nature was left to the mercy of American girls, which was professional duty rather than education as long as diplomacy held its own." During the years spent in Washington and Cambridge after his return, he never mentions the sex. As far as the pages of his *Education* are concerned he might have been living in a masculine world entirely bereft of women. Possibly both his shyness in life and his reticence in recording had each something to do with the production of this effect.

Nevertheless, the influence of his marriage, a singularly happy one to a remarkable woman, must assuredly have been of deep influence upon such a nature as Adams's, capable of deep affection and strongly loyal in his personal relationships. He himself never gave any written reference to his marriage, a gap of twenty years occurring in his *Education* from 1871 to 1892, covering the entire period of his married life, his wife's sudden and tragic death on December 6, 1885, and the period of wandering following that event. It is noteworthy in studying Adams's mind and life that the two women who had been closest to him, sister and wife, both met, in different ways, deaths almost equally tragic and unexpected. We shall not here lift the veil that Adams himself always held over his grief and shall confine ourselves to facts already scattered in print, for the most part, covering the years that he himself failed to record.

Granted a year's leave of absence from Harvard following his marriage he took his bride abroad and remained a year, on his return moving into the house in Boston at 91 Marlboro Street. In 1877, on Adams's retirement from his double posts of professor and editor, he and his wife moved to Washington and settled in "Corcoran's White House, next his own," on Lafayette Square, maintaining also a country home at Beverly, on the Massachusetts coast. In Washington the Adamses, the John Hays and Clarence King became inseparable, the three men with Mrs. Adams and Mrs. Hay being dubbed "the five of hearts." Mrs. Adams was a woman of rare charm and mind, and her drawing room became the most distinguished *salon* that Washington has ever held. Her influence on her husband's work was felt in many ways. A friend said that she told him that she had once stirred Adams into a spasm of activity by telling him how many candles Bancroft had used while writing before breakfast, and on one of their trips to Europe, gathering material for his historical writing in foreign archives, she would make requests that Adams himself was too shy to bring forward. She is said to have had "charm, intelligence, vivacity, tact, readiness and a keen mind," and to have been a distinguished *raconteur*. She daily read both Greek and Spanish with her husband. Before starting on their first trip to Europe, she had been given such flattering letters of introduction that she felt she could not present them but would read them over before the fire when she wished to cheer herself up. Her dinner table in Washington is reported to have been one of the most delightful to be found anywhere, and a frequenter recalls Adams, who had a keen sense of humor, "in uproarious laughter, waving his napkin up and down, at the stories told him by a clever woman" recounting her experiences on a Pacific coast ranch.[1]

The same friend speaks of the "singular charm" of the home at Beverly, and of the infectious air of "happiness, congeniality, and comradeship" there.

[1] Laughlin, cit supra.

One of Mrs. Adams's nieces wrote that "in the Beverly woods, a footpath, strewn with fragrant pine-needles, and bordered with ferns and lichened rocks, led to the Uncle's and Aunt's summer house. It was like having a private entrance into fairyland, and the Uncle and Aunt kept the keys and arranged the scenery. They had no children of their own, but they loved all young small things including dogs, and the dogs played an important part in their daily lives." The "nieces" recall him spending many hours in his den writing his *History,* clad "in cool white summer clothes—his fine head and thoughtful forehead dominated a small frame; his movements were deliberate—only the scratch of his pen would break the silence of the room until the delicious moment came when he would stop, and turn to them with an irresistibly droll remark." [1] The niece, Mrs. La Farge, also speaks of the impression conveyed by Adams and his wife of "oneness of life and mind, of perfect companionship."

[1] *Letters to a Niece,* Mabel La Farge, Boston, 1920, pp. 7ff.

Out of doors as in, they shared common tastes and both loved horseback riding, which they indulged on the roads through the Beverly woods. They were happy years and marked the beginning of Adams's most serious literary and scholarly work.

HISTORIAN AND NOVELIST

8.

HISTORIAN AND NOVELIST

THE dream of a newspaper career and of wielding power through the daily press had evaporated. Possessed now of a comfortable fortune, he devoted himself to gathering the materials for his monumental history of the administrations of Jefferson and Madison. In 1877 he edited the *Documents relating to New England Federalism, 1800-1815,* for which he wrote an introduction of only a few lines but gathered the documents illuminating one of the incidents in the career of his grandfather, John Quincy Adams. Two years later he published the three volumes of *The Writings of Albert Gallatin,* with a fourth volume of almost seven hundred pages containing the *Life,* Gallatin's son having placed an immense mass of material at Adams's disposal. As editor, Adams showed great restraint and published the *Writings* without annotation. Equal restraint, great balance and sense of proportion marked the *Life.* The refusal to obtrude the author's own predilections upon the reader was in marked contrast to the historical and biographical writing of the time, and the book became an authority at once, as it has since remained.

In 1880 an anonymous novel appeared, entitled *Democracy,* and although it at first attracted scant attention in America it became the talk of the season in London. Adams was in London that year but the mystery of the authorship was for long unsolved. The picture of social and political Washington presented in the book was quite evidently too intimate and understanding for anyone to have painted who was not of the inner circle. John Hay, Clarence King, Adams, Mrs. Adams and a number of others were suspected, but the truth about the authorship was not authoritatively given to the public until forty years after the appearance of the book. It was, of course, the work of Adams, Mrs. Adams contributing only an occasional description of a woman's costume. Adams wrote it, probably during 1878, and in the spring of the next year took the manuscript to Henry Holt, the New York publisher, who at once saw its value. At that time only King, Holt, Hay, Pumpelly and possibly Godkin were in the secret. The book cannot rank as a great novel but of its immense cleverness and interest there can be no doubt, and the picture of Washington in the late seventies and of American political life at that period almost makes of it an historical document. It has been said that the book was a "best seller" in its day. That is hardly true but it did sell well for an anonymous novel, fourteen thousand copies having been sold during the author's lifetime.

The next few years were very busy ones. Adams did not visit Europe again until 1892, and until his wife's death in 1885 must have kept very steadily at work in Washington and Beverly. In 1882 his

John Randolph was published in the excellent American Statesmen Series. Smaller in bulk and much lighter in style than the *Gallatin,* the book was more readable for the general public but the subject was not sympathetic to Adams. His book showed neither the mastery of facts nor the balance of judgment so apparent in the larger one, and the most recent life of Randolph, that by William C. Bruce,[1] should be consulted for a criticism of Adams's work. Adams himself did not like the book, in fact wrote that he detested it, and it is difficult to understand why he ever agreed to undertake it. About this same time he had also written a *Life of Aaron Burr,* but, according to Adams's own statement, it was declined by the publishers of the *Statesmen Series* on the ground that Burr was not a statesman. The manuscript was laid aside and has now disappeared.

Adams had evidently become interested in the novel as a form of expression and in 1884 published

[1] William C. Bruce, *John Randolph of Roanoke,* New York, 1922.

his second one under the pseudonym of "Frances Snow Compton." He himself and some of his family always considered *Esther* a better book than *Democracy* but it is difficult to share this opinion, and the public, knowing neither the real name of the author nor even that the new book was by the author of *Democracy,* wholly neglected it. It has been said that the book, for Adams, was peculiarly self-revealing, though the key to any personal disclosures is lost. Writing to Mrs. Don Cameron eight years after the book had appeared, and from far-away Tahiti, he declared that "I care more for one chapter, or any dozen pages of *Esther* than for the whole history, including maps and indexes; so much more, indeed, that I would not let anyone read the story for fear the reader should profane it . . ." [1] The unfinished sentence fails to reveal the source of the peculiarly intimate feeling Adams always retained for this one product of his pen. There were, however, almost as few readers as Adams himself would have wished, and even today

[1] *Letters,* cit supra, p. 468.

no copy is to be found in many of the leading libraries.

Adams's main preoccupation during these years was his *History of the United States* for which the *Gallatin, Documents relating to New England Federalism,* and *Randolph* had all been more or less preliminary studies. In 1884 he published in the *Revue Historique* in Paris an article on "Napoleon I at St. Domingo" which was also a by-product of his main work. He ransacked the foreign archives for material, as well as those in Washington, and, though Macaulay's style was quite different from his own, he read the famous history as a sort of stylistic tonic.

About this time he and John Hay bought the large corner property on H and 16th Streets, on the north side of Lafayette Square, for fifteen thousand dollars. Hay used the major portion of it for his house on the corner itself, and Adams planned a smaller house next door at 1603 H Street. Their friend, H. H. Richardson, was the architect of the two houses, which were started in the summer of

HOUSE OF HENRY ADAMS

1603 H. Street, Washington. Now torn down

1885. These Washington years were the happiest of Henry's life. Besides his smaller circle of intimates, such as the Hays, King, the Don Camerons and the Henry Cabot Lodges, Adams knew everyone whom he cared to know. The Lodges were old Boston friends, and Lodge had been one of his graduate students at Harvard. Cameron was Senator from Pennsylvania and with his brilliant and beautiful wife, a niece of Senator John Sherman, lived directly across the Square. Adams's work was going well, and to a great extent, although still loving irony and paradox, he had been brought out of the slough of too much introspection and self-depreciation in the congenial atmosphere in which he now lived. His love of fun and nonsense had full scope, as also his affection for children, which, although he never had any of his own, was always a marked characteristic. Those of the Camerons were welcome visitors and found an abundance of toys ready for them when allowed to run over to the Adams home. Suddenly, before the new house was finished, his life was snapped by the death of his wife under peculiarly tragic circumstances on December 6th. Adams moved into the new home alone but could not stand its solitude and in the following spring went on a long trip to Japan with his friend John La Farge, whose son Bancel later married Mabel Hooper, a niece of Mrs. Adams. A lasting memorial of this period is to be found in the brooding Oriental calm of the bronze figure over the grave of his wife and Adams himself in Rock Creek Cemetery of which we shall speak later.

Returning to Washington Adams resumed the task of completing his *History*. His nieces frequently visited him, and his friends rallied about him. Choice spirits came to his breakfasts which became an institution in Washington. Slowly but steadily the *History* proceeded. He had a considerable portion of it printed in an edition of six copies which he showed to a few intimate historical friends for criticism, among them his own brother Charles and George Bancroft, whose copies with their marginal notes are now in the Massachusetts Historical Society Library. The first completed two volumes were published in 1889; the next four in 1890; and the final three in 1891 after Adams had again gone to the East. The work at once placed Adams in the very first rank of American historians.

The first six chapters gave a masterly survey of the social, economic and other conditions in the United States in 1800 as an introduction to the main work. After forty years it yet remains unequalled for a picture of the national life, not only for that period but for any. In the remainder of the history the main stress is laid throughout on the political and diplomatic factors, a task for which Adams's inheritance, training and taste had all peculiarly fitted him. The long extracts from original documents which may occasionally weary readers who feel that they interrupt the flow of the narrative will for long make the volumes sources for the historian, but it is far from these alone to which the work owes its lasting value and interest. It is amazingly accurate, as impartial as a history of the period can be, and for the most part the style is that of a master of historical presentation. Many of the character sketches are inimitable, Adams showing much more ability in making his characters alive here than he had shown in his novels in which character was rather subordinated to cleverness of conversation and discussion. The author's sense of humor and irony stood him in good stead, and in the restrained form in which he here used them they give the effect of rumbles of Jovian laughter from Olympian heights above the wrangling struggles of disputatious mortals. For anyone whose intellectual fiber has not been weakened by a diet of "popular" history and biography, perhaps no other history of any American period affords such sheer intellectual delight. Certainly no other offers a more genuine contribution to historical scholarship and knowledge. At the time of the publication of the final volumes, another, containing the *Historical Essays,* was also published, consisting of reprints of many of his earlier articles, the only new one being "The Declaration of Paris, 1861."

Before these appeared, however, characteristically leaving his work to its fate among the reviewers,

Adams had again started for the Orient with La Farge. Some time before doing so he had commissioned Augustus Saint-Gaudens to design and cast the bronze memorial to Mrs. Adams. The sculptor worked hard to finish the work in clay before Adams left and did so but, again characteristically, Adams preferred not to see it until his return, saying that if he did not like it he would only carry disappointment throughout the trip and otherwise he would be able to anticipate pleasure.

By September 10, 1890, the two travellers were at Honolulu living in a house loaned them by a college classmate of Adams's, wearing Japanese kimonos and sketching, for Adams too had taken along a box of paints with which to amuse himself. By the middle of January, 1891, they were in Samoa, Adams playing with his sketches but learning a new appreciation of color from his own work and from La Farge. The 9th of February he was writing from Papeete, enjoying his leisurely travelling immensely. Early in April we can place him at Papara, Tahiti, expecting to sail about the 25th for

Fiji. The place evidently held them, however, for they did not sail until the 5th of June, arriving at Fiji on the 16th after a day's stop at Rarotonga. On September 10th he wrote that he and La Farge had "waltzed ahead, from one island to another, till I have to think a long time before I can remember where we are, when I wake in the night." Reaching Sydney they had gone to Brisbane by rail, then along the Australian coast by steamer to Batavia in Java, passing through Torres Strait and the Malay Archipelago, "four thousand miles of delightful travel, always in quiet water, generally in sight of land, and with lovely weather, moonlight nights, and a large, comfortable steamer." They spent a week in Java, visiting the interior of the island, and then proceeded from Batavia to Singapore, where they spent a couple of days, going thence to Ceylon. From Kandy they made an expedition to the ruined city of Anuradjapura where Adams sat under Buddha's Bo-tree and, as a result of that visit, wrote his poem, "Buddha and Brahma" while crossing the Indian Ocean. He wrote from Kandy to his niece that even if, in Ceylon, unlike Japan, he found Buddha rather a bore, he was glad to sit under his twenty-three hundred year old Bo-tree and attain perfection, although La Farge denied that he had done so. He did not visit India but sailed directly from Colombo to Marseilles, joining the Camerons at Paris and crossing to England with them while La Farge went to visit cousins in Brittany. November found Adams staying in Aberdeenshire with old friends, the Clarks, after a stop at Birmingham to see the Chamberlains. A brief trip to Paris, and he was soon back to Washington again.

While Adams was in the East, Saint-Gaudens had completed the monument which Adams had commissioned him to make for the grave of his wife. It is needless to give any fresh appreciation of Saint-Gaudens' masterpiece. The mood and thought for the figure had come to Adams in Japan on his first trip with La Farge, and after talking with the sculptor he had referred him to the artist and suggested that he should not study books but have about him photographs of Michael Angelo's frescoes in the Sistine Chapel at Rome and some pictures of Chinese statues, Buddhas and the like, which Adams sent to him. In his *Education* Adams has given his own interpretation of the monument. We may add that of Saint-Gaudens. In May, 1904, John Hay and Mrs. Barrett Wendell happened to meet the sculptor in the cemetery. Mrs. Wendell asked him what he called the figure. "He hesitated," she wrote in a letter, "and then said, 'I call it the Mystery of the Hereafter.'" To her further query, "It is not happiness?" he answered, "No, it is beyond pain and beyond joy."[1] In addition to what Adams wrote in the *Education,* we may also add an extract from a letter from him to Richard Watson Gilder in 1896. "The whole meaning and feeling of the figure," he wrote, "is in its universality and anonymity. My own name for it is 'The Peace of God.' La Farge would call it 'Kwannon.' Petrarch would say 'Siccome eterna vita è veder Dio,' and a real artist would be very careful to give it no name

[1] *The Reminiscences of Augustus Saint-Gaudens,* edited by Homer Saint-Gaudens, New York, 1913, vol. I, pp. 358ff.

that the public could turn into a limitation of its nature. With the understanding that there shall be no such attempt at making it intelligible to the average mind, and no hint at ownership or personal relation, I hand it over to Saint-Gaudens." [1]

Adams's first step after his return was to Rock Creek Cemetery to see the bronze, which wholly satisfied him, and thither he often went later to dream and ponder. "He supposed its meaning to be the one commonplace about it—the oldest idea known to human thought. He knew that if he asked an Asiatic its meaning, no man, woman, or child from Cairo to Kamchatka would have needed more than a glance to reply. . . . The interest of the figure was not in its meaning but in the response of the observer! As Adams sat there, numbers of people came, for the figure seemed to have become a tourist fashion, and all wanted to know its meaning. . . . None felt what would have been a nursery instinct to a Hindu baby or a

[1] *Ibid.*, p. 363. It is noteworthy that Adams quoted from this same sonnet of Petrarch in *Esther.*

Japanese jinriksha-runner." The clergy misinter-
preted it even worse than most.

The most profound work of art yet produced in
America, it has proved singularly baffling to the
matter-of-fact mind of most of those who visit it.
From the love of Adams and his wife, from the
brooding peace of the East to which Adams fled
from his tragedy, there has arisen amidst the most
frantic life of incessant practical activity that the
world has ever seen, the figure of eternal calm beyond desire. "Absorbed in revery . . . profound
assuagement emanates from her," writes the French
critic Gaston Migeon, who finds it the masterpiece
of modern art. But the American distrusts revery
and feels no need of assuagement. That all the
spiritual threads—the Boston heritage of Adams,
his submission to the Buddha and Kwannon of
Japan, the love that flowered between himself and
his wife, the French and Irish ancestry of Saint-
Gaudens, above all, the chaos of practical activity
and egoistic preoccupation of the America in which
they all lived as background—should have brought

THE ADAMS MEMORIAL
Rock Creek Cemetery, Washington
By Augustus St. Gaudens

forth, as the highest note ever touched in that nation, this figure of eternal calm, of utter selfless-
ness, transcends the utmost irony of which Adams
was ever capable.

AGE AND THE PHILOSOPHIC MIND

9.

AGE AND THE PHILOSOPHIC MIND

HIS *History* finished, as was also, next-door, Hay's *Life of Lincoln,* Adams and his small coterie sat watching life in Lafayette Square, the White House and the halls of Congress, with an amused detachment. The houses of the Hays, the Cabot Lodges, and the Camerons were second homes to the solitary Adams. Theodore Roosevelt, Cecil Spring-Rice and a few others were intimates. "The relation was daily, and the alliance undisturbed by power or patronage, since Mr. Harrison, in those respects, showed little more taste than Mr. Cleveland for the society and interests of this particular band of followers, whose relations with the White House were sometimes comic, but never intimate." The world was entering upon a new stage of mechanical power. Adams painfully learned to ride a bicycle.

In 1892, after having received the honorary degree of Doctor of Laws from Western Reserve University, he went to England to spend the summer on the Deeside, returning to Washington in October. The following February, 1893, he went with the Camerons to South Carolina, where they had bought an old plantation, and thence on to Havana, returning to stay on with the Camerons. With them also he went to the Chicago Exposition in May, and in June they all sailed for England, passing from there through France to Switzerland. At Lucerne, Adams found letters from his brothers urging his immediate return to Boston. The panic of 1893 had broken over the country. Free silver was not the only one of Adams's economic heresies. Cameron's views, and probably those of Brooks Adams, had greatly influenced him. In economics, even more than in science, Adams was an amateur but the economic pitfalls were perhaps the more dangerous for a novice, and his love of paradox served him ill in his discussion of such matters. We need not take his comments on the panic and his own relations to the banks very seriously. There was more truth in his statement that he found himself, on his return, "suspended, for several months, over the edge of bankruptcy." He reached Quincy August 7th; affairs improved; and the brothers weathered the financial storm. By September 19th Adams was back in his Washington home.

The Exposition at Chicago had so interested him that he soon started off for another fortnight there. His mind had now lain comparatively fallow for some years, and the display, not only of the unexpected beauty of the Exposition as an American and Western product, but of the new mechanical forces to be utilized by society, started his mind in the direction which it was to follow more or less for the rest of his life. "Men of science," he wrote, "could never understand the ignorance and naïveté of the historian, who, when he came suddenly on a new power, asked naturally what it was; did it pull

or did it push? Was it a screw or a thrust? Did it
flow or vibrate? Was it a wire or a mathematical
line?" "Did he himself quite know what he
meant? Certainly not! If he had known enough
to state his problem, his education would have been
complete at once. Chicago asked in 1893 for the
first time the question whether the American people
knew where they were driving. Adams answered,
for one, that he did not know, but would try to
find out." Practically the entire body of his later
work is here foreshadowed. Hereafter his main
preoccupation was to make a science of history, to
establish some sort of laws for the evolution of human society that should approach, as near as might
be, to mathematical precision.

The panic, which Adams had weathered, had
brought down Clarence King, who suffered a
physical as well as financial breakdown. In January, 1894, Adams took him to the West Indies for
the winter, and then went to the Yellowstone with
Hay for the summer. From there he went on alone
to Seattle and Vancouver, to look over more or less

the last important stretches of American railway which he had not yet seen. A letter dated at Washington, October 6th, shows that he must have been home then, but briefly, for he writes in the *Education,* "no sooner had he finished this debauch of Northwestern geography than with a desperate thirst for exhausting the American field, he set out for Mexico and the Gulf, making a sweep of the Caribbean and clearing up, in these six or eight months, at least twenty thousand miles of American land and water." By April, 1895, he was once more in Washington.

Meanwhile his new ideas on history had assumed their first form for publication. In 1891, when cruising the Pacific with La Farge, he had been elected a vice-president of the American Historical Association. He advanced through the usual routine of offices and in 1894 was president. Owing to his absence in Mexico he was unable to attend the annual meeting and to deliver the customary presidential address. In place of it he sent a communication in the form of a letter from Guadalajara which was published in the *Annual Report* with the title of "The Tendency of History." Brooks Adams says that Henry intended the essay originally as a sort of preface to Brooks's *Civilization and Decay* on which Brooks had for some time been working.[1] Henry pleaded for an attempt on the part of historians to place history on the footing of a science, even though failure was possible and perhaps probable. He pointed, however, to the danger. "What shape can be given to any science of history that will not shake to its foundations some prodigious interests?" "Any science of history must be absolute, like other sciences, and must fix with mathematical certainty the path which human society has got to follow." The dangers that historians would then meet from the opposition of great forces, such as the church, capitalism, the optimism of human nature, organized labor, or others to which the discovered laws might run counter, were plain.

For the members of the Association he merely

[1] *The Degradation of the Democratic Dogma,* edited by Brooks Adams, New York, 1919, p. 96.

posed the question, but it was clear in what direction his own thought was travelling. His mind was now taking great sweeps. In many respects his training had been remarkable. His work at Harvard had laid foundations, especially legal, far in the past. In Europe, notably in London, 1861-1868, and in Washington, he had closely watched history in the making from the inside; he had touched civilization again and again at its highest points in Europe; had seen human nature in low stages on its outer fringes in the Pacific islands; had come into contact with the ancient civilizations of the Far East in Japan and Ceylon; had read widely and thought profoundly. No one knew better than he that any generalizations to which his studies might lead him in the then knowledge of the science of society could be at best but tentative guesses, mere suggestions as to direction. Nevertheless, more than once such guesses of his were to prove remarkable as prophecies. At the present time there is a whole literature in Europe developing on the basis of the arrested development of that continent and of the danger to civilization of the swinging out of the orbit of Western European ideals on the part of Russia and America. Adams foresaw just such a possibility when pondering his "Tendency of History." Are we, he wrote in a letter to his brother Brooks, "on the edge of a new and last great centralization, or of a first great movement of disintegration? There are facts on both sides; but my conclusion rather is . . . that our so-called civilization has shown its movement, even at the centre, arrested. It has failed to concentrate further. Its next great effort may succeed, but it is more likely to be one of disintegration, with Russia for the eccentric on one side and America on the other." In view of the Great War and the Russian and American developments following it, few predictions thirty years in advance could be more accurate. At the time, however, Adams's essay was considered by most as the impractical dreamings of an amateur thinker, suggestive but not to be taken seriously. The next ten years Adams was to spend in travel, experience and reflection.

Herbert B. Adams Esq. Secretary &c.
American Historical Association.

Guadalajara. 12 December 1894

Dear Sir:

I regret extremely that circumstances should have prevented me from attending the meetings of the Historical Association. On the date which you have mentioned as that of its just biennial, I shall not be within reach. I have to ask you to offer my apology to the members, and the acknowledge that, at that moment, I am believed to be somewhere beyond the isthmus of Panama. Perhaps this ~~is~~ *absence runs* on some of the mysterious ways of nature's law, for you will not forget that, when you did me the honor to make me your President, I was still further away — in Tahiti or Fiji, I believe — and never even had an opportunity to thank you. Evidently I am ~~necessarily~~ ... may to be an absent President, and you will suffer ~~accordingly~~ *a defect* which is ~~not official, but~~ ... a condition of the mind.

I regret this fault the more because I would have liked to be of service, and

come, the Universities throughout the world
will have done most to create it, and are
under more obligation to find a solution
for it. I will not deny that the shadow
of this coming event has cast itself on me,
who is a teacher and to writers; so that, in
the last ten years, it has kept me silent where
I should once have spoken with confidence, or
has caused me to think long and anxiously
before expressing in public any opinion at all.
Beyond a doubt, silence is best. In these
remarks, which are only casual,
and of the paradoxical spirit
of a private conversation I have not ven-
tured to express any opinion of my own; or,
if I have expressed it, pray consider it
as withdrawn. The situation seems to call
for no opinion, unless we have some scientific
theory to offer; but to me it seems so interesting
that, in taking leave of the association, I feel
inclined to invite them as individuals to
consider the matter in a spirit that will

enable us, should the crisis arise, to deal
with it in a friendly temper, and a full
understanding of its serious dangers and responsibilities.

Ever truly yrs

Henry Adams

He set to work on new lines,—statistics, for one thing. The new trend of his thought and outlook on life that had slowly been developing was noted by himself. "The object of education, therefore," he says, "was changed. For many years it had lost itself in studying what the world had ceased to care for; if it were to begin again, it must try to find out what the mass of mankind did care for, and why." For the moment, he adds, he was rescued, as often, by a woman, and in the summer of 1895 Mrs. Cabot Lodge induced him to go abroad with her husband and sons. They were in England until the middle of September, Adams visiting old friends, and then crossed to France, where Adams began to see many things with fresh eyes. Amiens had never been "so marvellously perfect." They passed through Rouen and thence to Caen, Coutances, and Mont-Saint-Michel. Writing to Mrs. La Farge he said that the cathedral at Coutances "was something quite new to me, and humbled my proud spirit a good bit. I had not thought myself so ignorant or so stupid as to have remained blind to such things, being more or less within sight of them now for nearly forty years. I thought I knew Gothic. Caen, Bayeux, and Coutances were a chapter I never opened before. . . . The squirming devils under the feet of the stone Apostles looked uncommonly like me and my generation." The party passed two days at the Mont, "in the most abominable herd of human hogs I ever saw at the trough of a table d'hôte, but the castle was worth many hogs." He and the Lodges went on together to Paris (stopping at the Hotel des deux Mondes in the Avenue de l'Opéra), and there, as always, Adams found many friends, and too many Americans "sitting at every café, with penetrating voices proclaiming that they only wish they were in New York." A week of the interminable châteaux in Touraine followed, and then Adams was off to England again. At twenty-one he had claimed to detest everything French. Now he writes that "in spite of all its drawbacks, France has, still, more to give one than any other country has, that I know." Incidentally, the Lodges had enabled him to see the twelfth and thirteenth cen-

turies with fresh vision. He sailed for America
October 12th and "drifted back to Washington with
a new sense of history."

For months, however, he continued to wander.
First he went south, then in April (1896) to Mexico
again with the Camerons, only to start a few weeks
later, in May, back to Europe with John Hay, on
which trip he added Ravenna to his list of places.
By October they were once more in Washington
for the McKinley election. Adams had long been
interested in the Cuban problem, which was now
again nearing a crisis. He wrote a long article on
the question of recognition which, without, of
course, his name being attached, was presented as a
report to the Senate by Cameron in December.
McKinley, elected and inaugurated, named Hay as
ambassador to England, and by April 21, 1897,
Adams was there himself. He had a theory, which
he loved to expound, that a friend in office was a
friend lost, but he continued to drift with Hay. He
crossed, after a while, to Paris and remained there
until January, 1898, when, the Hays passing

through on their way to Egypt, they carried him along, to receive the news of the blowing up of the *Maine* while staying at Assouan. Adams speaks of this as his second trip to Egypt but I find no record of an earlier one save his cruising through the Red Sea and along the coast on his way back from the Pacific. From Cairo, leaving the Hays, "he went to Athens, picked up Rockhill, and searched for the harbor of Tiryns; together they went on to Constantinople and studied the great walls of Constantine and the greater domes of Justinian." Although his *Education* does not mention it, a letter reveals that he was also in Damascus. By spring he was back in England, where the Camerons had taken the fine old house of Surrenden Dering in Kent at which they, Adams, and frequently the Hays stayed during the summer, watching the events of the Spanish War and the new attitude of England toward America as a result of the German menace. Hay was recalled to become Secretary of State, and Adams, determined, he says, not to lose a friend without a struggle, returned also, settling once more into his house in Washington on November 13th.

Still his wanderings continued. The next spring, March 22, 1899, he sailed with the Lodges to spend April in Sicily and Rome. He passed a solitary summer in Paris and in November La Farge came along, leading him back once more to the twelfth century and to Chartres and its glass. The two friends came home together, reaching New York January 15, 1900, and Adams went on to Washington to look after Hay. There he again set to work at his historical problem,—how, this time, to bring the Washington of McKinley and Hay into some sort of mathematical relation with twelfth century Chartres, bringing them into some common relation. "All his associates in history condemned such an attempt as futile and almost immoral—certainly hostile to sound historical system." Ever since his early days with Lyell, science had fascinated Adams's mind. Throughout all his life he had played, fancifully or seriously, with evolution, with his *Pteraspis* and his *Terebratula,* until the latter were the most familiar symbols with which he dealt. Now he started afresh from a new standpoint— Willard Gibbs and his theory of Phase. Adams was never either a trained mathematician or a scientist. For him, as he said, "the details of science meant nothing: he wanted to know its mass." His interest was in the general principles and the philosophy. More and more he felt the need of bringing history into some sort of relation with the other sciences, of interpreting its data in terms of motion, direction, attraction, relation, of bringing the isolated facts into some kind of interpretive and predicable unity. By the 12th of May he was back in Paris in his rooms near the Trocadéro to study the exhibits at the Exposition. There, until January 19, 1901, when he sailed for home, he struggled with his problem.

"The historian's business," Adams felt, "was to follow the track of energy; to find where it came from and where it went to; its complex source and shifting channels; its values, equivalents, conversion." Studying the exhibits at the Exposition, the dynamo gave him one symbol and measure of force. But he instinctively felt that in history this was not all. Since 1895 "he had begun to feel the Virgin or Venus as force." "All the steam in the world could not, like the Virgin, build Chartres." To the working of his mind in the three years following the Exposition he has devoted a fifth of the whole of his *Education*. It is obviously unnecessary, therefore, to elaborate here. Before commenting on his next book, we need merely note that his travels continued. In 1901 he was in Europe again with the Lodges, revisiting Germany, going into Russia, and then, alone, to Norway and Sweden. Here, once more, he made a notable prediction. In 1901 he foresaw that "either Germany must destroy England and France to create the next inevitable unification as a system of continent against continent—or she must pool interests."

The pooling failed, and 1914 fulfilled Adams's prediction with almost scientific exactitude. For the remainder of his life, until the outbreak of the war thus predicted, which found him in France, he spent every summer there and it is unnecessary to chronicle each trip. For the most part they were for pleasure, not for study, and the curious in such matters may make out the dates, as well as may be, from the *Education* and from scattered letters. In 1904, before going to France as usual, he paid a brief visit to the Exposition at St. Louis.

Working out his theory of history, Adams had established in his mind two forces, which he represented by the Virgin and the dynamo, and it was probably about this time that he wrote the "Prayer to the Virgin," found in a little wallet after his death. To consider, however, force merely in itself could get one nowhere. One had to establish both motion and direction. As a working hypothesis to try out his theory and see whither it might lead, Adams decided to take two points between which he could trace the operation of force, and so possibly establish both a direction and a rate of acceleration. He chose as one point, that from which to start, the point at which, in his opinion, "man had held the highest idea of himself as a unit in a unified universe," which he located in the twelfth century. The other point was to be, for convenience, *himself*, as a symbol of twentieth century multiplicity. A complete analysis of the earlier century was thus his first task. This he performed in his book *Mont-Saint-Michel and Chartres,* in which, by analysis and synthesis, he has lit the clearest and most concentrated light to be turned upon the medieval period by any single volume in perhaps any language. Painting, glass, religion, poetry, architecture, philosophy, are here all primary colors in the combination of which Adams's conception shows in a brilliant white light. It is a book that could hardly have been written by anyone without his peculiar experiences of life. Into it went, not merely a lifetime of study, but long days, summer after summer, in the cathedrals; the Oriental sense of woman as one of the primal sources of nature, wholly alien to repressed and Puritan America; all that, among many things, La Farge, to whom Adams willingly acknowledged the deepest of debts, had taught him of color in Pacific sunsets and

Chartres windows; ponderings from under the Bo-tree of Anuradjapura and in the Machinery Hall of the Paris Exposition; the science of Willard Gibbs and the philosophy of Thomas Aquinas. Although written to establish a starting point for his theory of history it will probably be read most often as a unique expression of the soul of the period of which it treats.

Adams himself never made the slightest pretense to being an authority on any of the aspects of the time of which he wrote. Long past any desire for public recognition of any work of his, he had the volume privately printed in folio, in an edition of a few copies, of which he gave six to public libraries. The remainder he reserved for distribution among a few friends, and the edition was soon exhausted. After careful revision he again printed it privately, in 1912, but it was only with the greatest reluctance that he allowed the book, after constant insistence, to be published in 1913.

The establishment of a first point for his theory was, however, but half the work. His plan had called for two, between which "he hoped to project his lines forward and backward indefinitely," and to the establishment of this second point he now settled down again to work. The second point, as I have said, was to be himself as a symbol of twentieth century multiplicity. The result of his labor was *The Education of Henry Adams,* which he did not consider finished in the form in which it had finally to be given to the public after his death. Adams himself had no intention of writing merely an autobiography, though the book, when published, by others, had that as a subtitle. The establishing, however, of a second point, comparable to his first, for the purpose of his historical scheme, presented insuperable difficulties as he worked over it. He was, indeed, attempting what is, at the present at least, an impossible task. Like the *Chartres,* he published the book privately, in folio, 1907, limiting the edition this time to one hundred copies for his friends. If he failed in his effort to establish a point from which the forces of history might be calculated, he succeeded, without anticipation, in writing a unique book that will rank with the great autobiographies. Disregarding all requests to allow publication during his life, at his death he left the copyright to the Massachusetts Historical Society, and when published, first in a rather expensive, and later in a popular, edition, it met with an extraordinary sale.

Adams was now approaching seventy years of age. Without having at all a great fortune, he had the opportunity of gratifying every taste. Wherever he went, Washington, London, or Paris, he had a host of friends who gladly welcomed him. Of his circle in Washington an unnamed commentator wrote, after his death, that "between him and his younger friends there was a good understanding. Half of it was explicit—they were free to make use of his house, to bring anybody they pleased to luncheon, to give dinners there. By the terms of the other and tacit half they were to bring him, sooner or later, everybody in whose company he would find interest and pleasure. Fastidious all his life, at almost every contact with the world and with ideas, he was nowhere more fastidious than in choosing his acquaintance. And yet his friends seldom made a mistake about his taste. . . . Great names were nothing to his purpose. Neither large fortune, nor conspicuousness in political life, nor achievement in art or business could impose on him. . . . His was a social school where you had to take honors to pass."[1]

A niece writes of him at this period: "No one who loved him really feared him though his manner might be at times alarming to a stranger. His alternation of great gentleness with sudden brusqueness was temperamental and involuntary, and was part of his fascination. It made life exciting and varied in his presence. The brusqueness was nearly always to conceal a ray of tenderness that had escaped him." John Hay commissioned Saint-Gaudens to model a little caricature medallion of Adams's head with the body of a porcupine and the wings of an angel, and the inscription "Henricus Adams Porcupinus Angelicus." When Hay was ill

[1] *The New Republic,* May 25, 1928, p. 107.

and on his way to Nauheim, Adams cared for him
and Hay wrote to Saint-Gaudens that "he has been
kindness itself—the Porcupine has 'passed in music
out of sight' and the Angel has been perfected in
him," adding the verse

> *"Oh! Adams, in our hours of ease*
> *Rather inclined to growl and tease,*
> *When pain and anguish wring the brow*
> *A ministering angel thou."* [1]

Of his house, the commentator quoted above described it as "an odd home for such a fastidious man
as Mr. Adams. The leather chairs which abounded
were all so low that they seemed to have been made
for the host's own use. Things which he had
brought home from Europe and the East were
everywhere, and though they were beautiful their
total effect was not beauty but miscellaneousness.
To the eye it was a very Bostonian house, though
Mr. Adams did not care to have you think so."

In this environment, Adams continued to ponder

---

[1] *Reminiscences of Augustus Saint-Gaudens,* cit supra, vol. II,
p. 340.

JOHN HAY, IN 1902

over his theory of history. The old friends were going—Hay died in 1904 and Adams was to outlive King, but he continued to work. In 1908 he made the selection of Hay's letters which Mrs. Hay published in privately printed form, though he was not a little disconcerted when he saw the volumes to find that dashes had been substituted indiscriminately for all proper names. In 1909 he turned again to his historical writing with an essay on "Phase" which was not published until after his death by his brother Brooks in the volume, *The Degradation of the Democratic Dogma*. Based on Gibbs's theory of phase in physics, it was another attempt to correlate history with science. Using mathematical formulæ, the attempt appeared fantastic, yet the conclusion arrived at by the first calculation, that history would enter upon a new phase about 1917, has certainly had an astonishing, and at the time an unpredicable, confirmation.

In 1910 he published his scientific theories as to history, in a small but rather widely distributed pamphlet under the title of *A Letter to American*

Teachers of History. In this he again attempted to relate history to the sciences, mainly physics, and made much use of the law of entropy. All of Adams's writings on this subject were based, naturally, on the physical conceptions held twenty years or more ago. Since then physics, and indeed all scientific thought, have themselves entered upon a new "phase," which, rather curiously, became marked just about the time that the Great War inaugurated the new political phase, as Adams predicted. Not only did Bohr introduce the quantum theory of atomic structure in 1913 and Einstein extended the principle of relativity to a general theory in 1915, but the whole of the old Euclidean geometry, Newtonian physics, and the easily assumed mechanistic theory of the universe began to crumble. In 1930 one would be far less ready, and certainly feel far less scientific compulsion, to relate historic phenomena to the old physical categories of mass, direction, force, velocity, and so on than was the case in 1900-1910. In 1900 not only was unity and simplicity the goal but nothing else seemed conceivable. There appeared to be no option between invoking the supernatural or ultimately bringing thought and will under the laws of atomic physics as then understood. Today the situation is wholly different, and no one would have seized the new tendencies manifested, and intellectually played with all their possible implications for history, more avidly than Adams himself. His effort was to correlate history to the entire body of the most accurate and fundamental thought of his own day. If that thought has shifted ground it is not the fault of Adams, whereas the attempt to do exactly what he did will undoubtedly some day have to be undertaken again, that is, to correlate our historical knowledge with our other knowledge of the universe when that knowledge is sufficient. Even though there may be a shift in the ground, Adams will yet remain the first pioneer in a field which may be fertilized with greater knowledge but which will assuredly have no bolder or more brilliant cultivator.

The following year, 1911, Adams published his

Life of George Cabot Lodge, a tribute to the young poet who was one of his intimate circle; and also carefully revised his own *Chartres.* In the spring of 1912 he suffered a stroke of paralysis which ended his productive career and left him with impaired eyesight and diminished strength, although he recovered to so great an extent as to be able to enjoy life for the remaining six years and to continue his annual trips to Europe, spending his summers in France but also visiting other countries.

In the beginning of 1915, Henry Osborn Taylor sent Adams, who had long been a friend, a copy of his volume called *Deliverance.* In reply Adams wrote saying, "the early Christian faith I take to have been abandoned long ago by the failure of Christ to reappear and judge the world. Whatever faith is to save us, it cannot be that. Is it, then, the Stoic?" Had he been the author of Taylor's book, he added that he "should very likely have labored damnably over the Buddhists and the Stoics. Marcus Aurelius would have been my type of highest human attainment. . . . I need badly to find one man in history to admire. I am in near peril of turning Christian, and rolling in the mud in an agony of human mortification. All these other fellows did it,—why not I?"[1]

Stoicism or the Virgin? No one will know what the thoughts were that passed through the mind of the old man in the three years that were yet left. Marcus Aurelius was a far cry from William C. Whitney as the symbol of success a decade earlier, but, writing in 1915, Adams declared that he believed the "moral adjustment, as a story," ended there, and that at the most trying crisis of his life he had found only one support almost sufficient, that of Stoicism. It might be, he wrote, that that would be the faith to save us, which assuredly could not be that of the early Christians. The Virgin interested him as a force, but there were many forces,—the woman and the dynamo, love and electricity. The mystery deepened with the years, but it was in keeping with Adams's whole life that he

[1] Mss. letter, Henry Adams to Henry Osborn Taylor, Feb. 15, 1915.

should face the mystery courageously but unemotionally, erect and wrapped in the mantle of the Stoic rather than on his knees. In these last years he came to take delight in the old twelfth and thirteenth century songs, which he had sung to him every evening, and of which he accumulated a store in manuscript.

In August, 1914, he was living with his nieces in an old château in what had come to be his loved France when the storm of the Great War suddenly burst over the world. The old man's prophecies had been fulfilled, and returning to Washington, he watched from there and from various summering places the break-up of civilization which he had foreseen. He spent the evening of March 27, 1918, as usual with friends in his Washington home; listened to some of the medieval songs and retired to his room. "In the morning they found him asleep forever, with a look of thoughtful interest —almost of curiosity—upon his face." The following Saturday he was buried beside his wife, beneath Saint-Gaudens' symbol of the "Mystery of

the Hereafter," Adams's own "Peace of God," beyond pain, and beyond joy. In his Will he had
stated that other than that "no inscription, date,
letters or other attempt at memorial" should ever be
placed over their joint grave.

The education was finished.

BIBLIOGRAPHY

BIBLIOGRAPHY OF THE WRITINGS OF
HENRY ADAMS

1855

"Holden Chapel," *The Harvard Magazine*, May, 1855, vol. 1, pp. 210-215

"Resolutions on the Death of William Gibbons," *The Harvard Magazine*, December, 1855, vol. 2, p. 46

1856

"Resolutions on the Death of Hazen Dorr," *The Harvard Magazine*, June, 1856, vol. 2, p. 223

"My Old Room," *The Harvard Magazine*, September, 1856, vol. 2, pp. 290-297

Book Notice,—"Conquest of Kansas," *The Harvard Magazine*, November, 1856, vol. 2, pp. 395-396

Book Notice,—"Paul Fane," *The Harvard Magazine*, December, 1856, vol. 2, pp. 440-441

1857

"Retrospect," *The Harvard Magazine*, March, 1857, vol. 3, pp. 61-68

"College Politics," *The Harvard Magazine*, May, 1857, vol. 3, pp. 141-148

1857 *(continued)*

"Reading in College," *The Harvard Magazine,* October, 1857, vol. 3, pp. 307-317

"*ΚΑΤΟΙΗΣΙΣ ΚΕΙΛΕΙΑ,*" *The Harvard Magazine,* December, 1857, vol. 3, pp. 397-405

1858

"The Cap and Bells," *The Harvard Magazine,* April, 1858, vol. 4, pp. 125-132

1860

Letter, signed "H.B.A.," *Boston Courier*
    April 30
    May 9
    June 1
    June 29
    July 6
    July 10
    July 13
(The last two were reprinted, *American Historical Review,* January, 1920, vol. 25, pp. 240-255)

Letter, unsigned, *Boston Advertiser*
    December 10
    December 13
    December 20
    December 27

1861

    January 1
    January 11
    January 15

BIBLIOGRAPHY

1861 *(continued)*

January 16
January 17
January 22
January 24
January 26
February 2
February 6
February 8
February 11
Letter, unsigned, *New York Times*
June 3
June 7
June 17
June 21
June 28
July 4
July 15
July 19
August 2
August 12
August 15
September 6
September 14
September 24
September 26
October 8
October 13
October 20
October 28

1861 *(continued)*

November 2
November 7
November 18
December 19
"A Visit to Manchester. Extracts from a Private Diary,"
Boston Courier, December 16, 1861, unsigned

1867

"Captain John Smith," *North American Review,* January,
1867, vol. 1c4, pp. 1-30
"British Finance in 1816," *North American Review,*
April, 1867, vol. 104, pp. 354-386
"The Bank of England Restriction," *North American
Review,* October, 1867, vol. 105, pp. 393-434

1868

Between 1868 and 1870, Henry Adams appears to have
contributed book reviews and correspondence to *The
Nation* and *The New York Evening Post* but such
contributions cannot now be identified
A Review of Sir Charles Lyell's *Principles of Geology,
North American Review,* October, 1868, vol. 107, pp.
465-501

1869

"The Session," *North American Review,* April, 1869, vol.
108, pp. 610-640
"American Finance, 1865-1869," *Edinburgh Review,*
April, 1869, vol. 129, pp. 504-533

BIBLIOGRAPHY

1869 (continued)

"Civil Service Reform," *North American Review*, October, 1869, vol. 109, pp. 443-476. Published as a separate pamphlet, *Civil Service Reform by Henry Brooks Adams*, Fields Osgood & Co., Boston, 1869, 35 pp.

1870

"The Legal-Tender Act," by Francis A. Walker and Henry Adams, *North American Review*, April, 1870, vol. 110, pp. 299-327

"The Session, 1869-1870," *North American Review*, July, 1870, vol. 111, pp. 29-62

"The New York Gold Conspiracy," *Westminster Review*, October, 1870, vol. 38, pp. 411-436. Republished in *High Finance in the Sixties*. Yale University Press, 1929, pp. 120-155

1871

Chapters of Erie, and Other Essays, by Charles F. Adams and Henry Adams, James R. Osgood & Co., Boston, 1871, 2 p. 1, 429 pp. This volume contains three essays by C. F. Adams and five by Henry Adams. The latter, all reprints of those noted above, are: "The New York Gold Conspiracy," "Captain John Smith," "The Bank of England Restriction," "British Finance in 1816," and "The Legal-Tender Act." Reprinted in 1886

1872

"Harvard College," *North American Review*, January, 1872, vol. 114, pp. 110-147

1872 *(continued)*

"Freeman's Historical Essays," *North American Review*, January, 1872, vol. 114, pp. 193-196

"Maine's Village Communities," *North American Review*, January, 1872, vol. 114, pp. 196-199

"Denison's Letters and Other Writings," *North American Review*, April, 1872, vol. 114, pp. 426-432

"Howells' Their Wedding Journey," *North American Review*, April, 1872, vol. 114, pp. 444-445

"King's Mountaineering in the Sierra Nevada," *North American Review*, April, 1872, vol. 114, pp. 445-448

The Administration—A Radical Indictment! Its Shortcomings, Its Weakness, Stolidity. Thorough Analysis of Grant's and Boutwell's Mental Calibre. No Policy. No Ability. Washington, 1872. A reprint of "The Session" of July, 1870 *(vide supra)*, published as a campaign document by The National Democratic Executive Resident Committee, 16 pp.

"Holland's Recollections of Past Life," *North American Review*, April, 1872, vol. 114, pp. 448-450

1874

"Freeman's History of the Norman Conquest," *North American Review*, January, 1874, vol. 118, pp. 176-181

"Coulange's Ancient City," *North American Review*, April, 1874, vol. 118, pp. 390-397

"Saturday Review Sketches and Essays," *North American Review*, April, 1874, vol. 118, pp. 401-405

"Sohm's Procedure de la Lex Salica," *North American Review*, April, 1874, vol. 118, pp. 416-425

1874 *(continued)*

"Stubbs' Constitutional History of England," *North American Review*, July, 1874, vol. 119, pp. 233-244

"Kitchen's History of France," *North American Review*, October, 1874, vol. 119, pp. 442-447

Syllabus. History II. Political History of Europe from the 10th to the 15th Century. Cambridge, 1874, pp. i, 6. Reprinted, *Syllabus. History II. Political History of Europe from the Tenth to the Fifteenth Century.* Unpaged, 2 leaves only. Mss. date January 24, 1878

1875

"Parkman's Old Régime in Canada," *North American Review*, January, 1875, vol. 120, pp. 175-179

"Von Holst's Administration of Andrew Jackson," *North American Review*, January, 1875, vol. 120, pp. 179-185

"Clarke's Building of Brain," *North American Review*, January, 1875, vol. 120, pp. 185-188

"The Quincy Memoirs and Speeches," *North American Review*, January, 1875, vol. 120, pp. 235-236

"Bancroft's History of the United States," *North American Review*, April, 1875, vol. 120, pp. 424-432

"Maine's Early History of Institutions," *North American Review*, April, 1875, vol. 120, pp. 432-438

"Palgrave's Poems," *North American Review*, April, 1875, vol. 120, pp. 438-444

"Green's Short History of the English People," *North American Review*, July, 1875, vol. 121, pp. 216-224

"Tennyson's Queen Mary," *North American Review*, October, 1875, vol. 121, pp. 422-429

1875 *(continued)*

"Palfrey's History of New England," *North American Review,* October, 1875, vol. 121, pp. 473-480

1876

"Von Holst's History of the United States," by Henry Adams and Henry Cabot Lodge, *North American Review*, October, 1876, vol. 123, pp. 328-361

"The Independents in the Canvass," *North American Review,* October, 1876, vol. 123, pp. 426-467, by Henry Adams and C. F. Adams, Jr.

Essays in Anglo-Saxon Law, edited by Henry Adams, Little, Brown & Co., Boston, 1876. The first of the four essays, "The Anglo-Saxon Courts of Law" (55 pp.), is by Henry Adams. Reprinted 1905.

"Primitive Rights of Women" was delivered as a Lowell Lecture on December 9, 1876, but apparently not printed until published in revised form in the *Historical Essays* in 1891.

1877

Documents Relating to New England Federalism, 1800-1815, edited by Henry Adams, Little, Brown & Co., Boston, 1877, xi, 437 pp. Reprinted 1905.

1879

The Writings of Albert Gallatin, edited by Henry Adams, 3 vols., J. B. Lippincott, Philadelphia, 1879

The Life of Albert Gallatin, J. B. Lippincott, Philadelphia, 1879, v, 697 pp.

BIBLIOGRAPHY

1880

Democracy,—An American Novel (published anonymously), Henry Holt & Co., New York, 1880, 1 p. 1, 374 pp. (*Leisure Hour Series,* No. 112), reprinted many times. There were 9 printings of the 1880 Holt edition, issued in two bindings at $1.10 and $1.00 respectively. In 1882 a cheap edition went through five printings. In 1885 it was again issued by Holt in their *Leisure Moment Series.* There were three printings of their 1902 edition which contained some changes. In 1925 it was republished by Holt, pp. vii, 374, with a Foreword by Henry Holt. Republished Macmillan & Co., London (1882), 2 p. 1, 280 pp.; Ward, Lock & Co., London (1882), 186 pp.; Tauchnitz edition, Leipzig, 1882.

There was also a French edition: *Démocratie, roman Américain,* Plon & Cie., Paris, 1883, jésus, viii, 324 pp. Although dated 1883 either the volume or a title page had been received by the *Bibliographie* by November 28, 1882.

1881

Pocahontas and Captain Smith, by "H. A.," Q. P. Index, Bangor, Maine, published September 10, 1881. (*The Monograph: A Serial Collection of Indexed Essays,* No. XIX) 8vo. Also, undated but with the imprint, A. William & Co., Boston, and A. Brentano, New York.

1882

John Randolph, Houghton Mifflin Company, Boston, 1882, vi, 313 pp.; 1898, 5 p. 1, 326 pp. (*American Statesmen Series.*)

1882 *(continued)*

At this period Adams had written at least part of a biography of Aaron Burr which now appears to have been lost or destroyed.

1884

"Napoleon at St. Domingo," published originally in French, *Le Revue Historique,* Paris, April, 1884, vol. 24, pp. 92-130

Esther,—A Novel, published under the pseudonym of Frances Snow Compton, Henry Holt & Company, New York, 1884, 1 p. 1, 302 pp. (*American Novel Series,* No. III). Richard Bentley & Son, Ltd., London, 1885

1885

History of the United States of America during the Second Administration of Thomas Jefferson—1805-1809. Privately printed Cambridge, John Wilson & Son, University Press, 1885, viii, 601 pp. Six copies only.

1888

History of the United States of America during the First Administration of James Madison—1809-1813. Privately printed Cambridge, John Wilson & Son, University Press, 1888, ix, 535 pp. Six copies only.

1889

History of the United States of America during the First Administration of Thomas Jefferson, 2 vols., Charles Scribner's Sons, New York, 1889

BIBLIOGRAPHY

1890

History of the United States of America during the Second Administration of Thomas Jefferson, 2 vols., Charles Scribner's Sons, New York, 1890

History of the United States of America during the First Administration of James Madison, 2 vols., Charles Scribner's Sons, New York, 1890

1891

History of the United States of America during the Second Administration of James Madison, 3 vols., Charles Scribner's Sons, New York, 1891

The above nine volumes were reprinted with an introduction by Henry Steele Commager in 4 volumes as *The History of the United States during the Administration of Thomas Jefferson,* 2 vols., and *The History of the United States during the Administration of James Madison,* 2 vols., by Albert & Charles Boni, Inc., New York, 1930

Historical Essays, Charles Scribner's Sons, New York, 1891, 2 p. 1, 422 pp. This volume contains the following nine essays, all of which except numbers 1 and 6 had been previously published (*vide supra*):

1. Primitive Rights of Women
2. Captain John Smith
3. Harvard College, 1786-1787
4. Napoleon at St. Domingo
5. The Bank of England Restriction
6. The Declaration of Paris, 1861

1891 *(continued)*

7. The Legal-Tender Act
8. The New York Gold Conspiracy
9. The Session, 1869-1870

1893

Memoirs of Marau Taaroa, Last Queen of Tahiti, privately
printed, no place, 1893, 109 pp. (Two copies in the
Massachusetts Historical Society.)

1895

"The Tendency of History," American Historical Association *Report* for 1894, pp. 17-23, Washington, 1895;
"The Tendency of History" was also issued as a separate pamphlet in an edition of 50 copies which was
found entire in the original package after the death
of Henry Adams, he never having given away a single
copy. These are now among his papers in the Massachusetts Historical Society. Republished, The Macmillan Co., New York, 1928, 4 p. 1, 3-175 pp., diagrams.
It was republished by The Book League of America,
New York, 1929, 175 pp.

"Count Edward de Crillon," *American Historical Review,*
October, 1895, vol. 1, pp. 51-69

1896

"Recognition of Cuban Independence," printed as *Senate
Report No. 1160 of the 54 Cong., 2d. Sess.,* Dec. 21,
1896, and submitted to the Senate by Senator Don
Cameron, pp. 1-25 of the *Report*

BIBLIOGRAPHY

1901

Memoirs of Arii Taimai E. Marama of Eimeo Teriirere of Toorai, Terrinui of Tahiti, Tauraatua E. Amo, edited and translated by Henry Adams. Half titles, *Travels, Tahiti.* Privately printed, Paris, 1901, 2 p. i, 196 pp. incl. vii geneal. Tab. An enlargement and revision of the Memoirs of Marau Taaroa (*vide supra*)

1904

Mont-Saint-Michel and Chartres, privately printed (150 copies only), Washington, 1904, copyrighted 1905, vi, 355 pp.

"King," in *Clarence King Memoirs,* published for the King Memorial Committee of the Century Association by G. P. Putnam's Sons, New York, 1904, pp. 157-185

1907

The Education of Henry Adams, privately printed (40 copies only), Washington, 1907, vi, 453 pp.

1908

Henry Adams selected the material for, but was not the editor of, *Letters of John Hay and Extracts from Diary,* printed but not published, Washington, 1908, 3 vols.

1910

A Letter to American Teachers of History, privately printed at the Press of J. H. Furst & Co., Baltimore, 1910, vi, 214 pp.

"Washington In 1861," written in 1861, published in 1910, Massachusetts Historical Society, *Proceedings,* vol. 43, pp. 656-689

1911

The Life of George Cabot Lodge, Houghton Mifflin Co., Boston, 1911, 3 p. 1, 206 pp.

1912

Mont-Saint-Michel and Chartres, privately printed in revised form, Washington, 1912, vi, 371 pp., illustrated

1913

Mont-Saint-Michel and Chartres, first published "by authority of the American Institute of Architects" through Houghton Mifflin Co., Boston, 1913, xiv, 401 pp.

1915

"Buddha and Brahma," a poem, *The Yale Review,* October, 1915, vol. 5, pp. 82-89

1918

The Education of Henry Adams,—An Autobiography, first published by the Massachusetts Historical Society in an edition of 250 copies for members. Published the same year by Houghton Mifflin Co., Boston (with different title page), x, 519 pp. (Popular edition, Houghton Mifflin Co., Boston, 1928, x, 517 pp.) Henry Adams wrote the Preface signed H. C. Lodge. Republished in *Modern Library,* New York, 1931, with Preface by James Truslow Adams, x, 517 pp.

1919

The Degradation of the Democratic Dogma, with an Introduction by Brooks Adams, The Macmillan Co., New York, 1919, xv, 317 pp. Republished 1920

1919 *(continued)*

Introductory Note, by Brooks Adams
The Heritage of Henry Adams, by Brooks Adams
The Tendency of History, by Henry Adams
The Rule of Phase Applied to History, by Henry Adams
Mont-Saint-Michel and Chartres, printed for Massachusetts Historical Society from the plates of 1913 after corrections in an edition of 250 copies, Boston, 1919, xiv, 401 pp.

1920

"Prayer to the Virgin of Chartres," probably written about 1904, first published in *Letters to a Niece, and Prayer to the Virgin of Chartres by Henry Adams with a Niece's Memories, by Mabel La Farge,* Houghton Mifflin Co., Boston, 1920, pp. 125-134

LIST OF WORKS IN WHICH MAY BE FOUND PERSONAL LETTERS FROM HENRY ADAMS

A Cycle of Adams Letters, 1861-1865, edited by Worthington C. Ford, Houghton Mifflin Company, Boston, 1920, 2 vols.

Garrulities of an Octogenarian Editor, Henry Holt, Houghton Mifflin Co., Boston, 1923

Letters to a Niece and Prayer to the Virgin of Chartres, by Henry Adams, with a Niece's Memories, Mabel La Farge, Houghton Mifflin Co., Boston, 1920

HENRY ADAMS

The Letters and Friendships of Sir Cecil Spring-Rice,
edited by Stephen Gwynn, Houghton Mifflin Co.,
Boston, 1929.

Letters of Henry Adams, edited by Worthington C. Ford,
Houghton Mifflin Co., Boston, 1930

The Reminiscences of Augustus Saint-Gaudens, edited
and amplified by Homer Saint-Gaudens, Century Co.,
New York, 1913, 2 vols.

Life of Whitelaw Reid, Royal Cortissoz, Charles Scribner's Sons, New York, 1921, 2 vols.

Early Memories, Henry Cabot Lodge, Charles Scribner's
Sons, New York, 1913

"Henry Adams, '58," James Ford Rhodes, *The Harvard
Graduates Magazine,* vol. 26, 1917-1918

The Degradation of the Democratic Dogma, edited by
Brooks Adams, The Macmillan Co., New York, 1919

"Seventeen Letters of Henry Adams," edited by Frederick
Bliss Luquiens, *The Yale Review,* October, 1920, vol.
10

"Six Letters of Henry Adams," edited by Albert Stan-
burrough Cook, *The Yale Review,* October, 1920, vol.
10

"Three Letters of Henry Adams," edited by A. S. Cook,
The Pacific Review, September, 1921, vol. 2

John La Farge, A Memoir and a Study, Royal Cortissoz,
Houghton Mifflin Co., Boston, 1911

"The Education of Henry Adams," Henry Osborn Taylor, *The Atlantic Monthly,* October, 1918

Letters of John Hay, and Extracts from Diary. Printed
but not published, Washington, 1908, 3 vols.

BIBLIOGRAPHY

Life and Letters of E. L. Godkin, Rollo Ogden, The Macmillan Co., New York, 1907, 2 vols.

The Adams Family, James Truslow Adams, Little, Brown & Co., Boston, 1930

Human Values and Verities, Part I, Henry Osborn Taylor, privately printed, n.p., 1929. [Note: This volume should not be confused with the same author's *Human Values and Verities,* published by Macmillan & Co., London, 1928.]

INDEX

INDEX

Aberdeenshire, 165

Adams, Abigail Brown, 26

Adams, Abigail Smith, 22, 29

Adams, Brooks, 226, 227, 228; views on Henry Adams, 28, 107; rooms with Henry, 129; economic views, 176; concerning "The Tendency of History," 180; letter to, 182

Adams, Charles Francis (1807-1886), 26-27; writings, 27, 44; minister to England, 31, 74; elected to Congress, 73; in London after the Civil War, 95, 98-99

Adams, Charles Francis, Jr., 47, 65, 160; in the army, 83; post-war career, 114, 115; writings, 120, 217, 220; advice to Henry, 125, 136

Adams, Edith Squire, 19

Adams, Hannah Bass, 20

Adams, Henry, the earliest recorded Adams, 19, 60

Adams, Henry [Brooks],

Works projected, *preface;* birth, 17; ancestry, 17-35; influences moulding his career and psychology, 17-35, 39, 43-45, 79; writings, 18, 63, 69, 86-90, 97-110, 118-124, 131, 134, 146, 151-162, 167, 180, 203-206, 213-229; as seen by Brooks Adams, 28, 107; "power" motive, 31-33, 50, 54, 61, 83-85, 97, 102, 104, 109-110, 151; boyhood, 39-50; oration at Harvard, 49, 56; career problem, 49-50, 61, 95-110; travel, 50, 54-67, 99, 122-123, 160, 163-167, 176-179, 187-194; youth, 53-69; destiny, 55; art, 56, 60, 62, 64, 163, 187, 195; æsthetics and intellect, 65-67, 107, 166-169; amateur diplomat, 73-91; views on England in the Civil War, 86-90; journalistic projects and work, 98, 101-107, 113-125; affection

INDEX

INDEX

INDEX

INDEX

INDEX

INDEX

INDEX

INDEX

INDEX

Squire, Edith (*see* Adams, Edith Squire)
Stoicism, 206, 207
Sturgis, Ellen (*see* Hooper, Ellen Sturgis)
Sturgis, Mrs. Russell, 141
Sturgis, William, 139
Sumner, Charles, 61, 77-79; influence on Henry Adams, 43, 44, 48
Sun, New York, 117
Sweden, 193
Switzerland, 176; impression on Henry Adams, 63
Sydney, Australia, 164
Syllabus, History II, etc., Henry Adams, 219

Tahiti, 155, 163
Taylor, Henry Osborn, *preface,* 132, 133, 134, 206, 207 *note,* 228, 229
Taylor, Zachary, 46
"Tendency of History, The," Henry Adams, 180, 182, 224
Tennyson, Alfred Lord, 44
Thackeray, William Makepeace, 44
Thoron, Mrs. L. H., *preface*
"Three Letters of Henry Adams," Cook *editor,* 228
Thun, Switzerland, 63
Thuringia, 62
Times, London, 77, 88, 89, 98
Times, New York, 87, 90, 117, 215

Tiryns, Greece, 190
Tocqueville, Alexis de, 101
Torres Strait, 164
Touraine, 188
Tribune, New York, 117

United States, career opportunities compared with England, 33-35; in 1868, 113-114

Vancouver, B. C., 178
Venus, as a symbol and power, 65, 192
Victoria, Queen, 34
Vienna, Congress of, 85
Virgin, as a symbol and power, 65, 192, 207
"Visit to Manchester, etc., A," Henry Adams, 216

Wagner, Richard, 59
Walker, Francis A., 119, 217
Washington, George, 22, 46
Washington, D. C., 129, 142, 181, 198; visited in 1850, 45-46; in 1860, 73; Henry Adams's feeling for, 115; journalism in, 116-122; in *Democracy,* 152, 153; Henry Adams's historical researches in, 156; Henry Adams's home, 159, 160, 165, 176, 179, 189, 191, 208
"Washington in 1861," Henry Adams, 225
Webster, Daniel, 26, 43

INDEX

15.5
17 ⟌265
  17
  /95
  85
  /100